SHRED Guitar

A Guide to Extreme Rock and Metal Lead Techniques

by Greg Harrison

ISBN 978-1-4234-2493-2

HAL•LEONARD® CORPORATION
7777 W. BLUEMOUND RD. P.O. BOX 13819 MILWAUKEE, WI 53213

In Australia Contact:
Hal Leonard Australia Pty. Ltd.
4 Lentara Court
Cheltenham, Victoria, 3192 Australia
Email: ausadmin@halleonard.com

Copyright © 2009 by HAL LEONARD CORPORATION
International Copyright Secured   All Rights Reserved

No part of this publication may be reproduced in any form or by any means
without the prior written permission of the Publisher.

Visit Hal Leonard Online at
www.halleonard.com

Contents

	Page	Track
About This Book	4	
About the Author	4	
Acknowledgments	4	
Chapter 1: **Tone/Technique/Warm Up**	5	1–3
Chapter 2: **Practice Techniques/Speed Development**	11	4–9
Chapter 3: **Three-Note-Per-String Blues Scales and Partial Picking**	18	10–15
Chapter 4: **Sweep Picking Part 1**	23	16–23
Chapter 5: **Sweep Picking Part 2**	31	24–31
Chapter 6: **Economy Picking**	37	32–40
Chapter 7: **String Skipping**	41	41–48
Chapter 8: **Tapping**	48	49–55
Chapter 9: **Extended Arpeggios**	55	56–68
Chapter 10: **Odd Groupings/Hybrid Picking**	60	69–83
Chapter 11: **Wide-Stretch Licks**	66	84–95

About This Book

This book was written for anyone who wants to take his or her chops to the next level. We'll be covering warm ups, practice techniques, speed picking, sweep picking, legato, wide stretch licks, string skipping, hybrid picking, and odd groupings. To get the most from this book, I strongly recommend that you make up your own variations and write some music with these concepts. Be creative!

About the Author

Greg Harrison began playing guitar in Wilmington, Ohio at the age of 15. He grew up listening to all styles of music, but the aggressive sound of metal lit a fire in him. At 22, Greg moved to Hollywood to attend Musicians Institute, where he formed the bands Shredzilla and P.D.P. He won the GIT Outstanding Stylist award in 2004 and started teaching at MI shortly after. Greg has performed guitar for video games, done numerous guitar clinics, and toured on the Mayhem festival 2008/2009 doing guitar clinics for *Revolver* magazine. As well as maintaining a full teaching schedule at MI, Greg can be found performing with his band P.D.P. all around LA. His influences include, but are not limited to, Pantera, Jason Becker, George Bellas, Paul Gilbert, Racer X, and Meshuggah. He uses Lance Alonzo custom guitars, Bill Lawrence pickups, Gotoh hardware, Randall and Krank amplifiers, and MXR and Dunlop pedals. You can check out Greg's music at pdpmusic.com, myspace.com/heavyocity, and myspace.com/shredzilla3.

Acknowledgments

I would like to thank all my friends, family, and students for their inspiration and support! (Special thanks goes to Bill LaFleur for telling me to get this thing published!)

Tone/Technique/Warm Up

Tone

I'm going to talk about tone first. There are many factors that make up one's personal guitar tone; they include the type of guitar, pickups, amp, effects pedals, and of course, your hands. It's a good idea to find a guitarist whose tone you really dig and try to imitate it. Remember, crappy tone will not help motivate you!

Let's look at two guitarists with great tone that sound nothing alike: Dimebag Darrell and Yngwie Malmsteen. Dimebag Darrell (of Pantera) used Dean ML guitars equipped with high output Humbucking pickups (Bill Lawrence/Seymour Duncan pickups), through rack gear that contained all kinds of EQs, as well as a bunch of pedals. He also used solid state (no tubes) Randall amps for most of his career; the bass is heavy, the highs are cutting, and the midrange is pretty heavily scooped in certain spots of the frequency spectrum. His sound was super focused and punishing—nothing pretty about it! Yngwie Malmsteen, on the other hand, uses a Fender Stratocaster guitar equipped with single coil pickups, Marshall tube amps, and various overdrive and delay pedals to deliver his brand of shred. His guitar sound has a lot of highs and midrange with less bass. Yngwie's sound isn't nearly as focused or punishing as Dime's, but his tone is no less influential or inspiring.

I prefer "The Dime" sound for my personal use, but I also use a Strat quite frequently. Try using these guidelines to help you sculpt your own tone. A great guitar tone will make listening to yourself a pleasure, not a pain!

Technique

There are many different schools of thought when it comes to the topic of "proper" technique. I will offer my insight, but by no means are these concepts the ONLY way to play. Everyone's hands are different, thus, there are different techniques.

The Pick Hand

First, let's have a look at the pick hand. I hold the pick firmly on the side of my index finger with my thumb (Fig. 1:1).

Fig. 1:1

The degree of pick angle I use to strike a string will change depending on if my thumb is bent (more angle) or straight (less angle). The angle depends on what I want the string to sound like when it's attacked. Aggressive metal rhythm guitar sounds great with a lot of angle on the low strings (Fig. 1:2). This will supply ample grit.

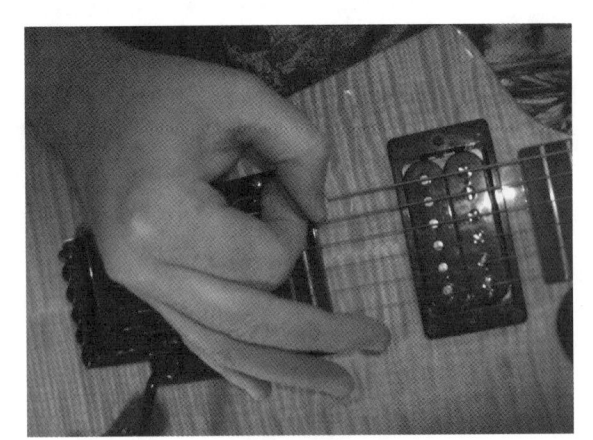

Fig. 1:2

Fast picking on the high strings sounds great with the pick at about a 45-degree angle (Fig. 1:3).

Fig. 1:3

Positioning of the fingers on your pick hand is also important. When playing rhythm on the low strings, I allow my pick-hand fingers to touch the strings I'm not picking. This helps to ensure no unintentional notes are sounded (Fig. 1:4).

Fig. 1:4

When I'm playing lead, I tend to make a loose fist when playing notes on the high strings so that my pick hand fingers are out of the way (Fig. 1:5). Make sure to keep your pick hand and arm relaxed to maintain control, and hold the pick only tight enough so you won't drop it—relaxation is the key here.

Fig. 1:5

Chapter 1

The Fret Hand

Now let's check out the fret hand. There are two basic ways to place your hand: the blues position and the classical position. The blues position is usually used for bending, while the classical position is friendly for fast passages and wide stretches.

The blues position is achieved by hooking your thumb over the top of the fretboard—similar to the way you would hold a baseball bat (Fig. 1:6). This provides ample leverage to dig in and bend the hell out of the strings.

Proper classical position entails placing the thumb of your fret hand in the middle of the back of the guitar neck (Fig. 1:7). Make sure your palm doesn't touch the fret board, and keep your fingers curled to avoid hitting multiple strings unintentionally.

Fig. 1:6

Fig. 1:7

Warm Up

Before you begin any kind of focused practice, it's important to warm up—it helps to avoid injury and frustration. Here are a few simple warm-up exercises to get your fingers and mind cooperating. These exercises are aimed at synchronization, not speed. Take your time, and focus on playing them cleanly—remember to stay relaxed.

The first exercise is a four-note-per-string, quasi-chromatic warm up (Fig. 1:8). Try this one legato (with hammer-ons and pull-offs) as well as with alternate picking (consistent, down/up/down/up picking pattern).

Track 1

Fig. 1:8

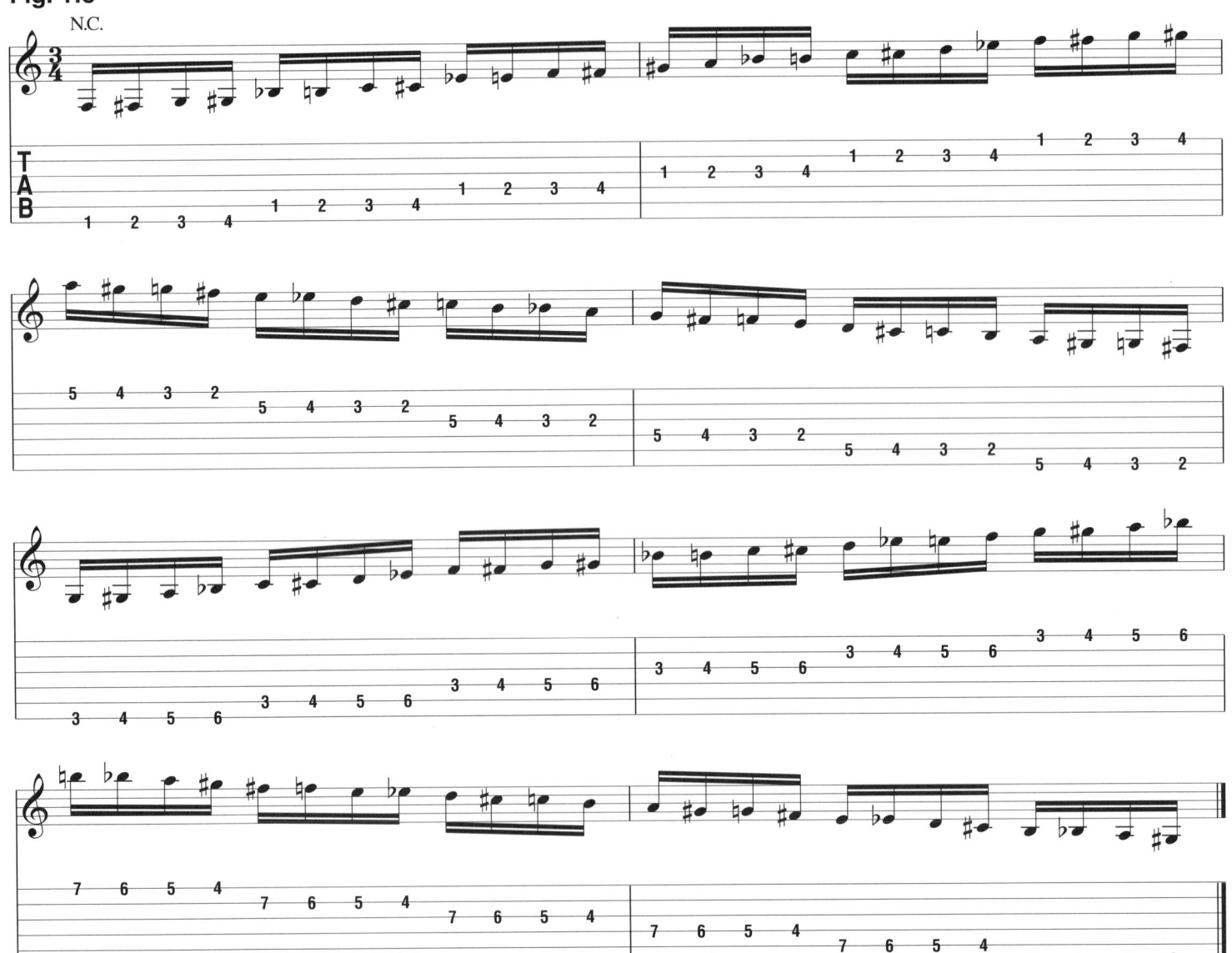

This next warm-up (Fig. 1:9) consists of seven, three-note-per-string patterns of the C major scale (C–D–E–F–G–A–B). Keep in mind, these patterns can also be used for the relative A minor scale (A–B–C–D–E–F–G).

Track 2

Fig. 1:9

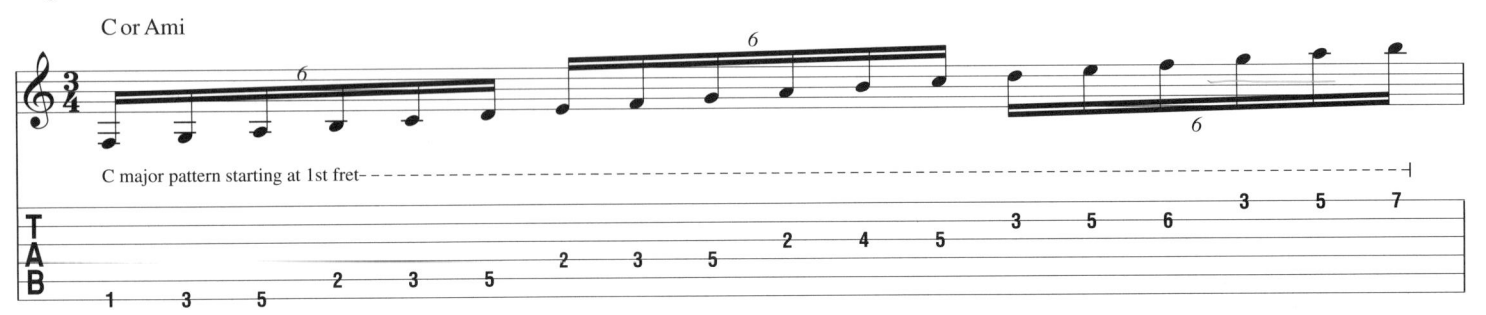

C or Ami

C major pattern starting at 1st fret

Chapter 1

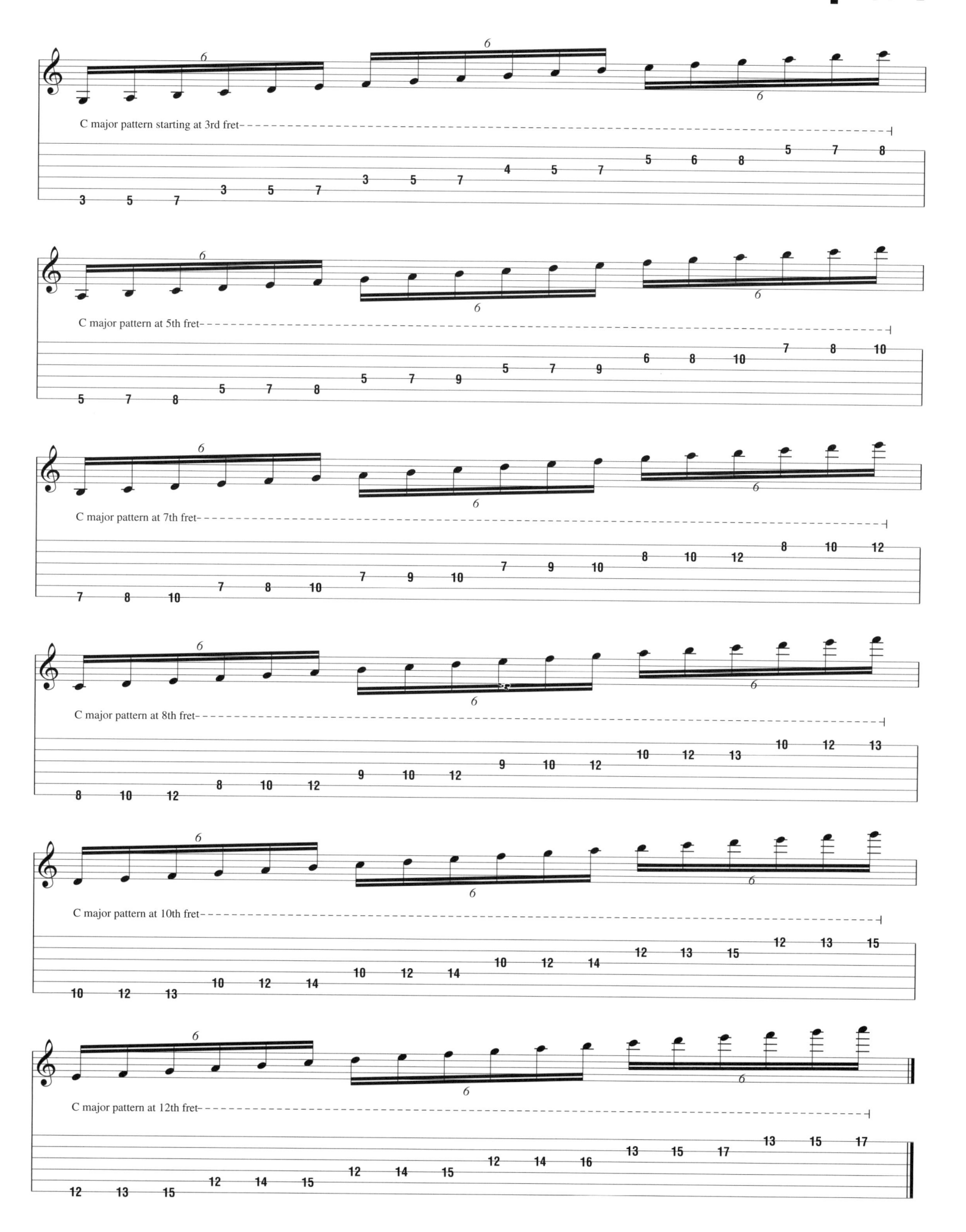

After these scale patterns are under you fingers, try connecting them by playing up one pattern, then shifting up one position to descend through the next, as shown here in Fig. 1:10.

Track 3

Fig. 1:10

C or Ami

2 Practice Techniques/Speed Development

First, a few words on how to get the most out of this book. When doing any of the exercises, perform them slowly and perfectly at first—don't race through each example. Gradually move through each lesson, making sure that it is thoroughly ingrained and completely understood. A good target speed is 120 bpm for groups of six (sextuplets), and 160 bpm for sixteenth notes. We must first build a good technical foundation before moving on to more advanced concepts which can, and will, expose weaknesses. Let's start with the basics of speed picking.

Here's an exercise on a single string (Fig. 2:1). Let's first perform the lick with only the fretting hand. Start by hammering-on (from mid-air) to the 5th fret of the high-E string, and then hammer-on to the 7th and 8th frets, then pull-off to the 5th fret where the pattern begins again.

Track 4
(0:00)

Fig. 2:1

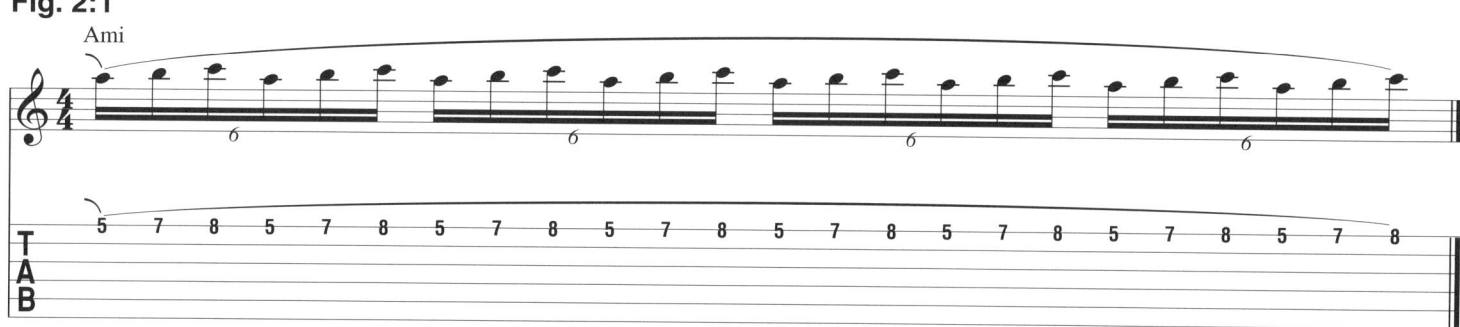

Now, we'll isolate the pick hand by playing the rhythm of the example on the open high-E string, using alternate picking (Fig. 2:2).

Track 4
(0:05)

Fig. 2:2

By practicing each part separately (left and right hand), we can now understand which part is more difficult. If one hand cannot perform the lick individually, practice this until synchronization is no longer a problem. Try applying this concept to every example and you'll see the method to the madness.

Practice the following examples (Figs. 2:3–2:8) with both alternate picking and legato techniques. If you encounter synchronization issues, try applying the isolation methods we just discussed.

11

The next two examples illustrate two different picking approaches to the same three-note-per-string lick. If you start the lick with a downstroke, the highest note will be plucked with an upstroke (Fig. 2:9A). If you start with an upstroke, the highest note will be a downstroke (Fig. 2:9B).

Track 5
(0:00)

Fig. 2:3

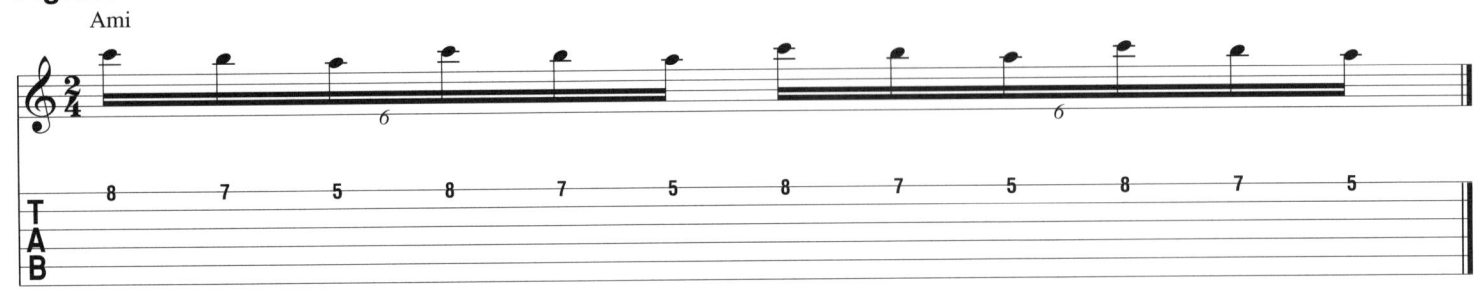

Ami

2/4

```
8 7 5  8 7 5  8 7 5  8 7 5
```

Track 5
(0:04)

Fig. 2:4

Ami

4/4

```
8 7 8 5  8 7 8 5  8 7 8 5  8 7 8 5
```

Track 5
(0:10)

Fig. 2:5

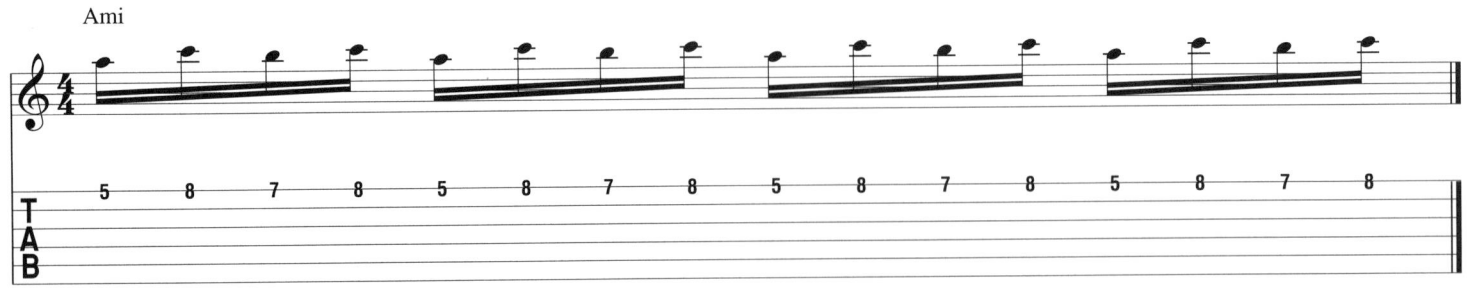

Ami

4/4

```
5 8 7 8  5 8 7 8  5 8 7 8  5 8 7 8
```

Track 5
(0:16)

Fig. 2:6

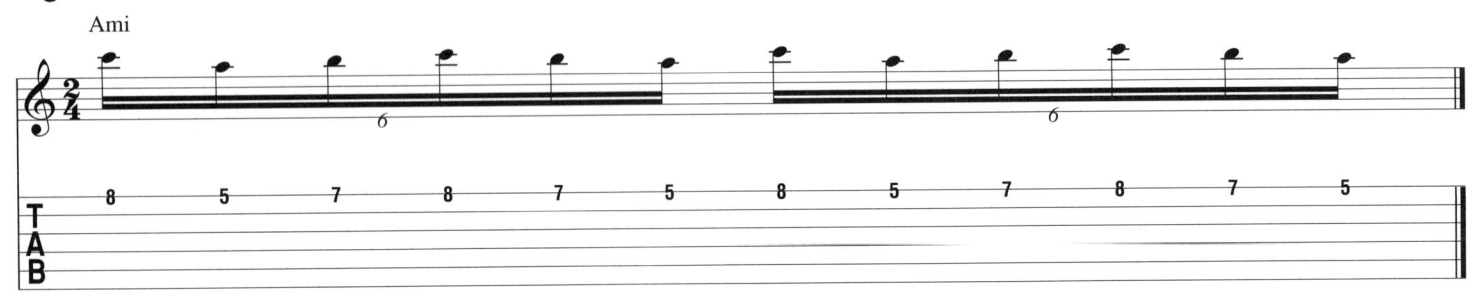

Ami

2/4

```
8 5 7 8 7 5  8 5 7 8 7 5
```

12

Chapter 2

Track 5
(0:20)

Fig. 2:7

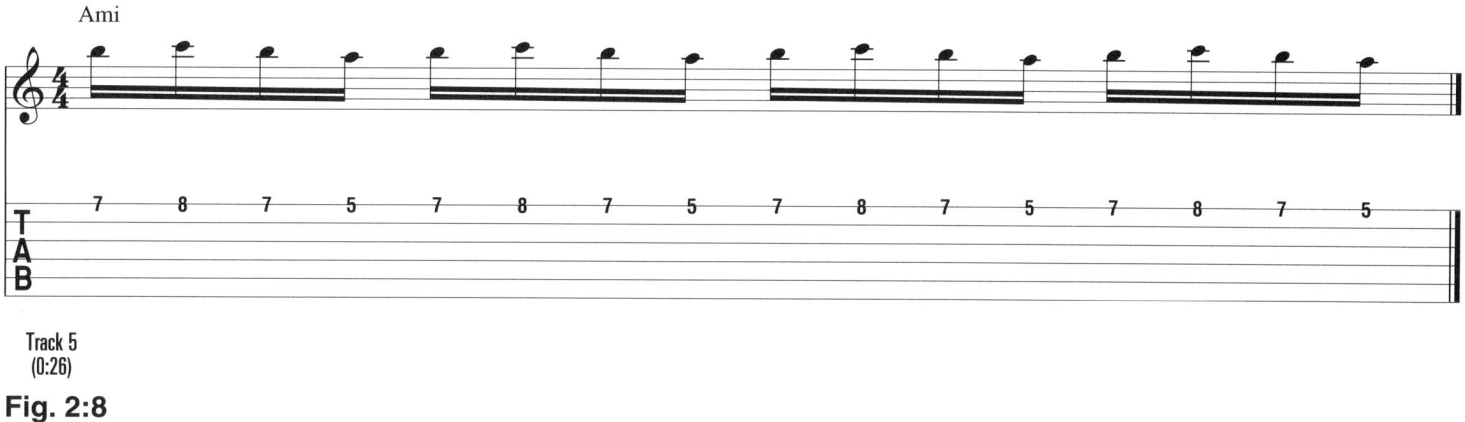

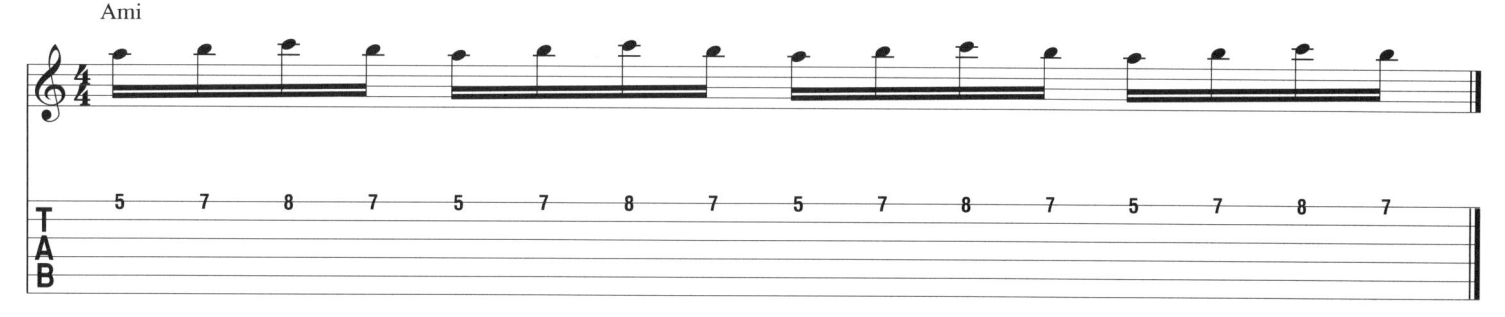

Ami

Fig. 2:8 follows with Ami.

Track 5
(0:26)

Fig. 2:8

Ami

Fig. 2:9A is an example of "outside picking;" Fig. 2:9B is "inside picking." Most likely, one will feel more comfortable to you, but favoring one over the other can create problems executing certain phrases. Try to practice both techniques to the point where they are equally strong.

Track 6

Fig. 2:9A

⊓ = downstroke
∨ = upstroke

Emi

⊓ ∨ ⊓ ∨ ⊓ ∨ simile

Fig. 2:9B

Emi

∨ ⊓ ∨ ⊓ ∨ ⊓ simile

Here is a variety of examples you can use to hone your "inside" and "outside" picking techniques (Figs. 2:10–15). Remember to start slowly and precisely, gradually increasing your speed only after you've mastered each one at a slower tempo. Also, feel free to cycle each lick several times in a row. For the sake of continuity, all are in the key of E minor. After you have them under your fingers, try transposing them to other keys.

Track 7 (0:00)

Fig. 2:10

Track 7 (0:06)

Fig. 2:11

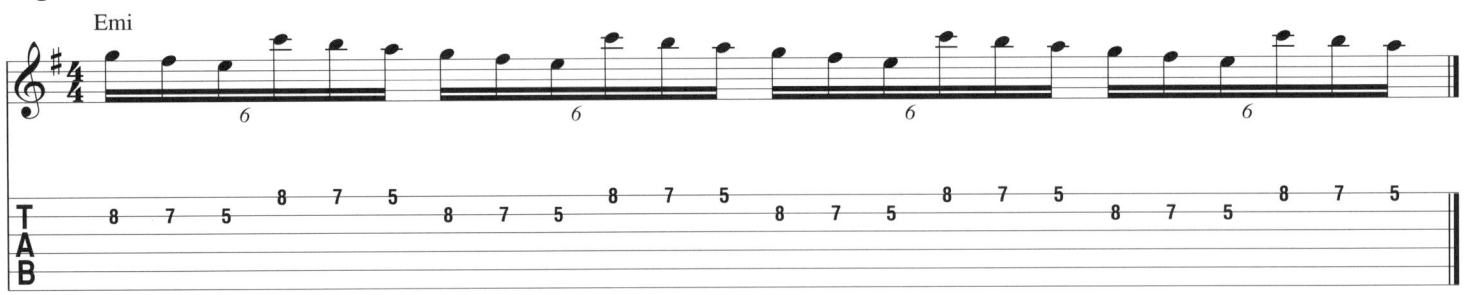

Track 7 (0:12)

Fig. 2:12

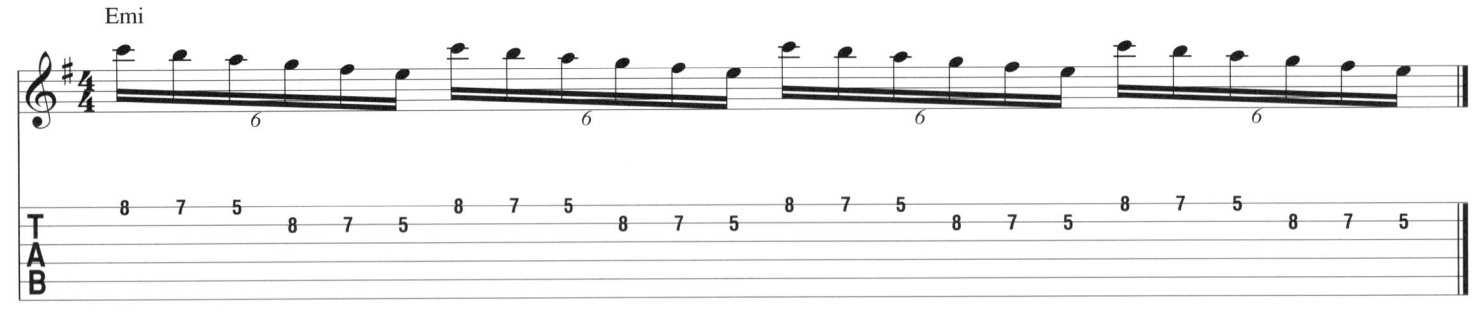

Track 7 (0:18)

Fig. 2:13

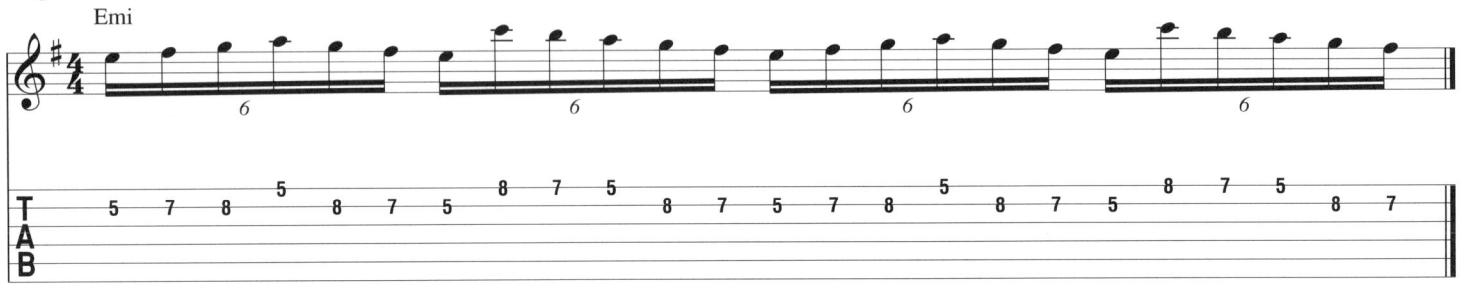

14

Chapter 2

Track 7
(0:24)

Fig. 2:14

Track 7
(0:30)

Fig. 2:15

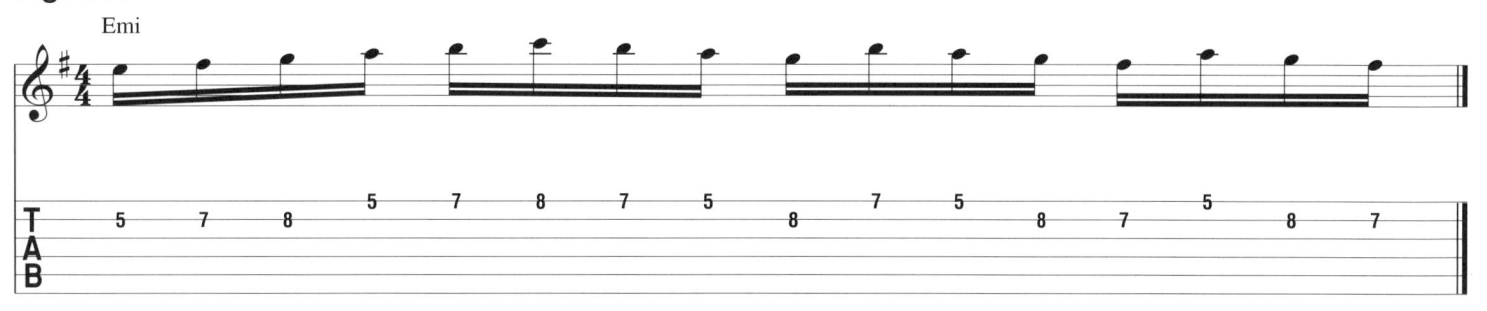

The next two examples require a position shift back-and-forth from the 5th fret to the 7th (Figs. 2:16–17).

Track 8
(0:00)

Fig. 2:16

Track 8
(0:06)

Fig. 2:17

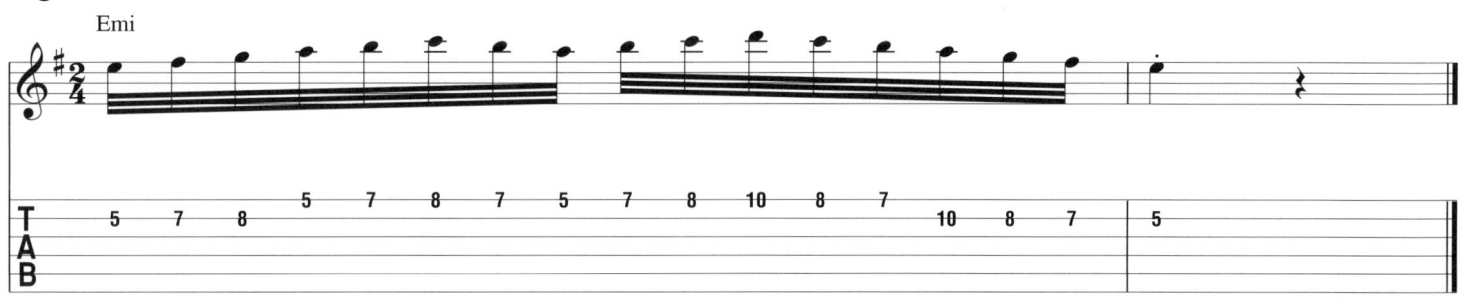

15

2

We're going to close this chapter with an etude in A minor (Fig. 2:18). Based on chords harmonized from the A minor scale (A–B–C–D–E–F–G), each one-bar section is modal by nature. We start with A Aeolian (modal name for the A minor scale) in the first measure, and move to A harmonic minor (A–B–C–D–E–F–G♯) in the second. Measure 3 follows a three-note, scalar motif in G Mixolydian (G–A–B–C–D–E–F; fifth mode of C major) that segues to D Mixolydian (D–E–F♯–G–A–B–C; fifth mode of G major) for a gradually-ascending, six-note sequence. Measure 5 reverts back to G Mixolydian for a pedal-tone oriented passage. The final three measures are based on Phrygian dominant sequences and scale passages. (Phrygian dominant is the fifth mode of the harmonic minor scale.) C Phrygian dominant (C–D♭–E–F–G–A♭–B♭; fifth mode of F harmonic minor) supplies the foundation for measure 6, B Phrygian dominant (B–C–D♯–E–F♯–G–A; fifth mode of E harmonic minor) snakes its way through measure 7, and the etude goes out on a descending E Phrygian dominant (E–F–G♯–A–B–C–D; fifth mode of A harmonic minor) phrase. Put the etude together slowly, measure-by-measure, until you have it at a respectable tempo, then get a friend to play the chords while you shred.

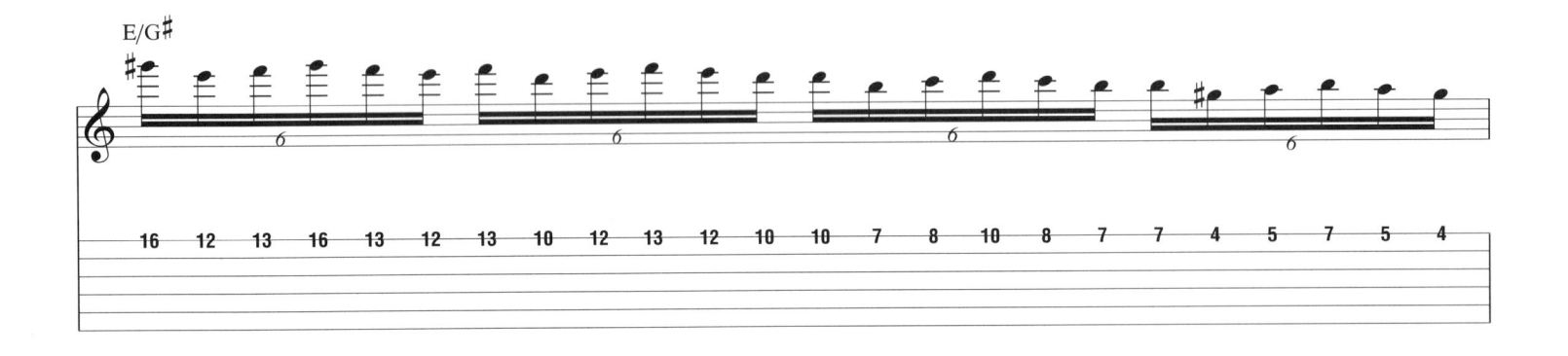

Track 9

Fig. 2:18

Chapter 2

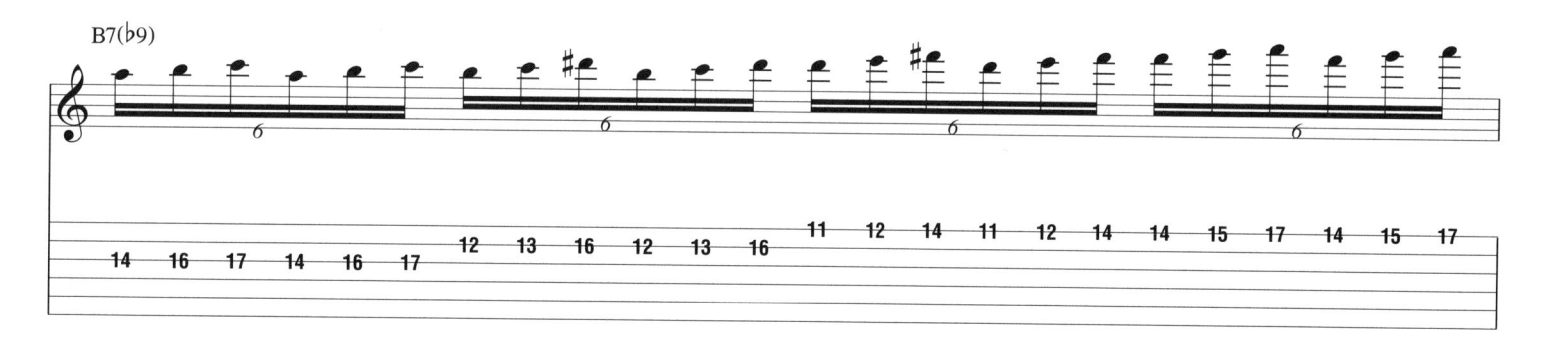

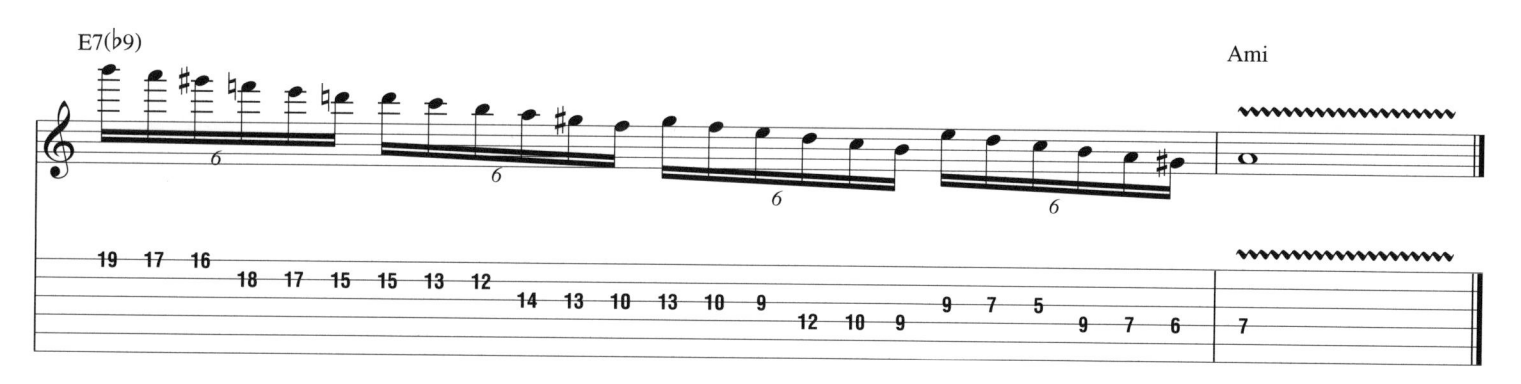

3 Three-Note-Per-String Blues Scales and Partial Picking

The blues scale (1–♭3–4–♭5–5–♭7) is one of the most widely used scales in improvisation. Our goal is to update some of the fingerings to make them more applicable to the shred approach. Let's look at some three-note-per-string examples.

Fig. 3:1 shows a three-note-per-string, A blues scale (A–C–D–E♭–E–G) pattern. Notice there are some pretty wide stretches. For those areas, try either a "1–2–4" or a "1–3–4" fret-hand fingering pattern.

Track 10

Fig. 3:1
A Blues

```
e|-----------------------------------------11-12-15-|
B|--------------------------------10-13-15----------|
G|-----------------------8--9--12-------------------|
D|--------------7--10-12----------------------------|
A|------6--7-10-------------------------------------|
E|-5-8-10-------------------------------------------|
```

Fig. 3:2 is a three-note-per-string pattern for the D blues scale (D–F–G–A♭–A–C). Again, experiment with different fret-hand fingering combinations for the wide stretches.

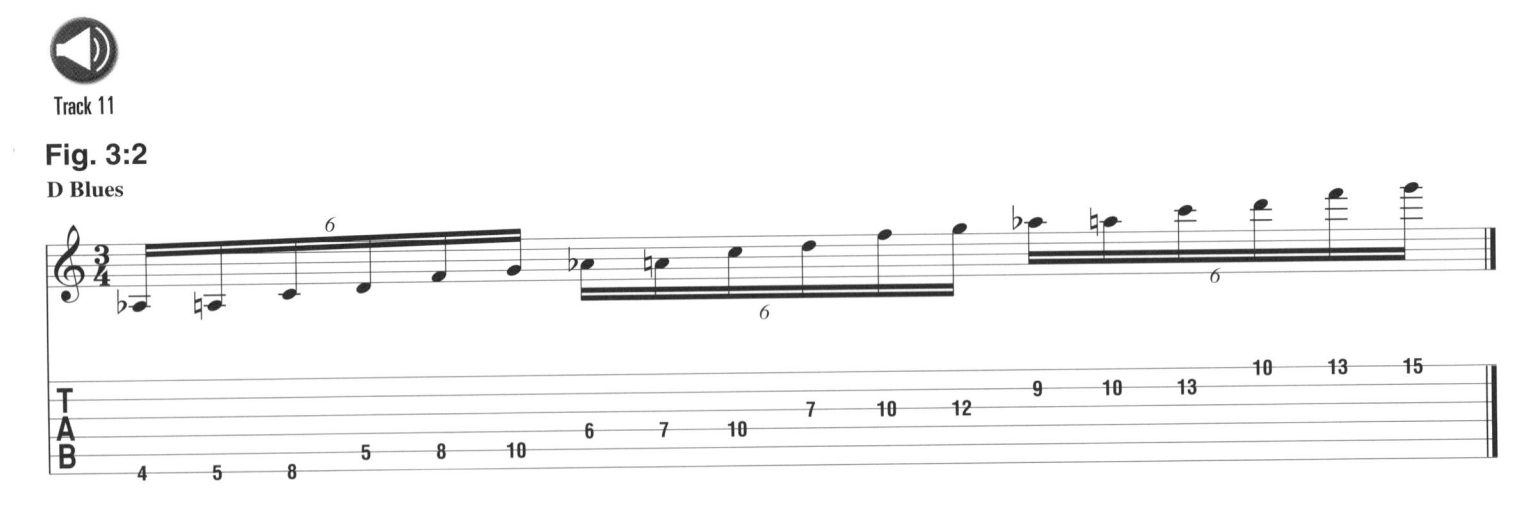

Track 11

Fig. 3:2
D Blues

```
e|--------------------------------------10-13-15-|
B|-----------------------------9-10-13-----------|
G|-------------------7-10-12---------------------|
D|-----------6-7-10------------------------------|
A|----5-8-10-------------------------------------|
E|-4-5-8-----------------------------------------|
```

Laying out the blues scale in such a manner allows us to apply the same speed-picking and legato techniques addressed in the previous chapter. Let's check out a few examples.

18

Chapter 3

Fig. 3:3 zips across the entire A blues scale pattern via a gradually ascending sequence.

Track 12 (0:00)

Fig. 3:3

A5 or A7

```
5 8 10  6 10 8  5 8 10  6 7 10  7 10 12  8 12 10  7 10 12  8 9 12
```

```
10 13 15  11 15 13  10 13 15  11 12 15  17
```

This A blues scale example follows a six-note sequence up the high-E string (Fig. 3:4).

Track 12 (0:08)

Fig. 3:4

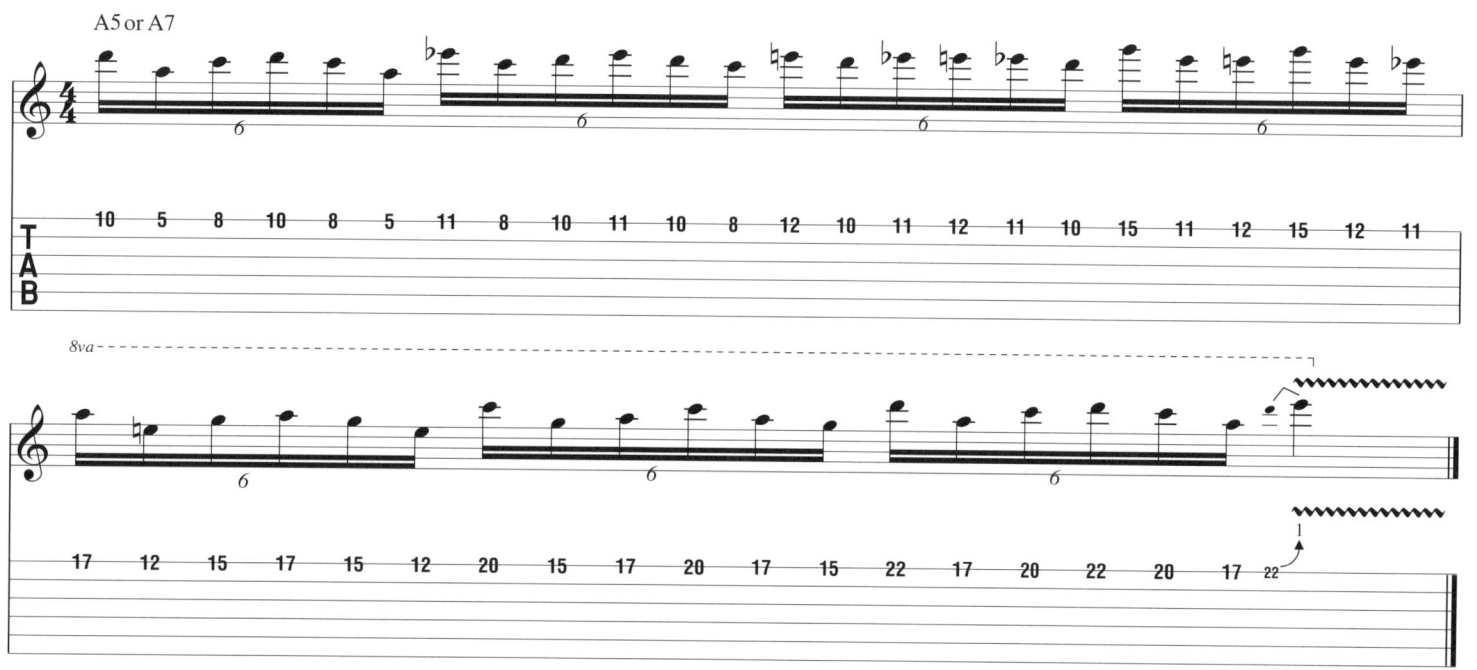

A5 or A7

```
10 5 8 10 8 5  11 8 10 11 10 8  12 10 11 12 11 10  15 11 12 15 12 11
```

8va

```
17 12 15 17 15 12  20 15 17 20 17 15  22 17 20 22 20 17  22
```

19

3

The next few examples explore a technique referred to as partial picking—or picking mixed with legato. Used by Eddie Van Halen and Dimebag Darrell, the technique offers greater speed, and a more fluid (yet still aggressive) sound. The first (Fig. 3:5) crosses the A blues scale pattern courtesy of a three-note sequence that is played twice on each string. The first cycle is picked, while the second is played using hammer-ons.

Track 13 (0:00)

Fig. 3:5

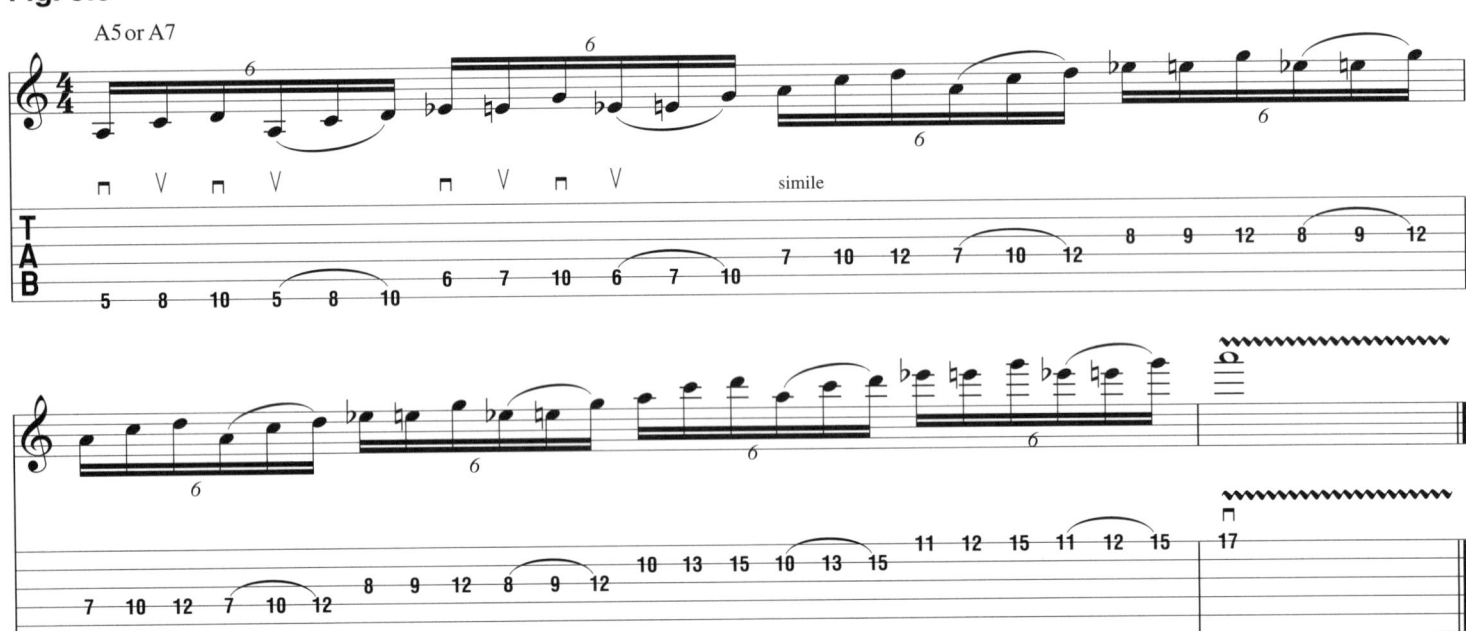

Fig. 3:6 isolates the low-E and A strings of the A blues scale pattern.

Track 13 (0:10)

Fig. 3:6

20

Chapter 3

The next two partial-picking examples are carved from the D blues scale pattern from Fig. 3:2.

Track 14
(0:00)

Fig. 3:7

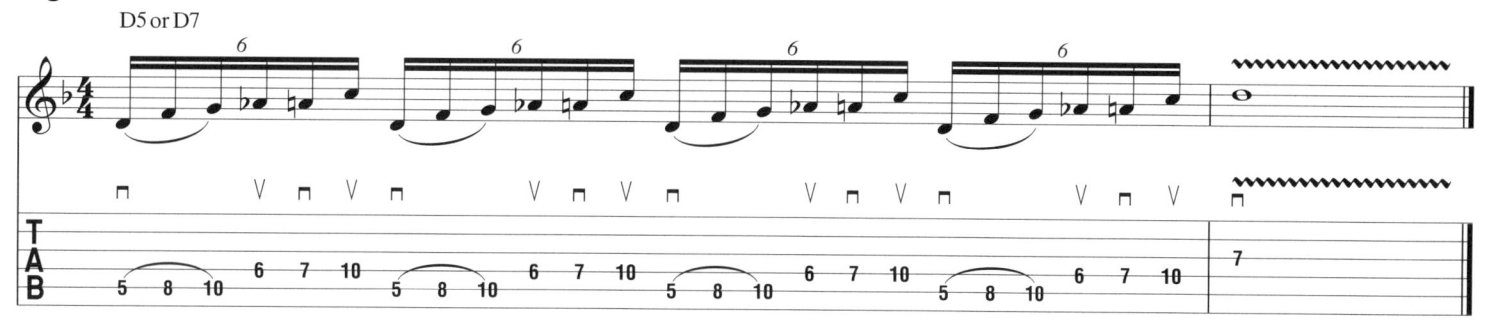

Track 14
(0:08)

Fig. 3:8

Here's a burning A blues scale example played on the high-E string (Fig. 3:9).

Track 14
(0:16)

Fig. 3:9

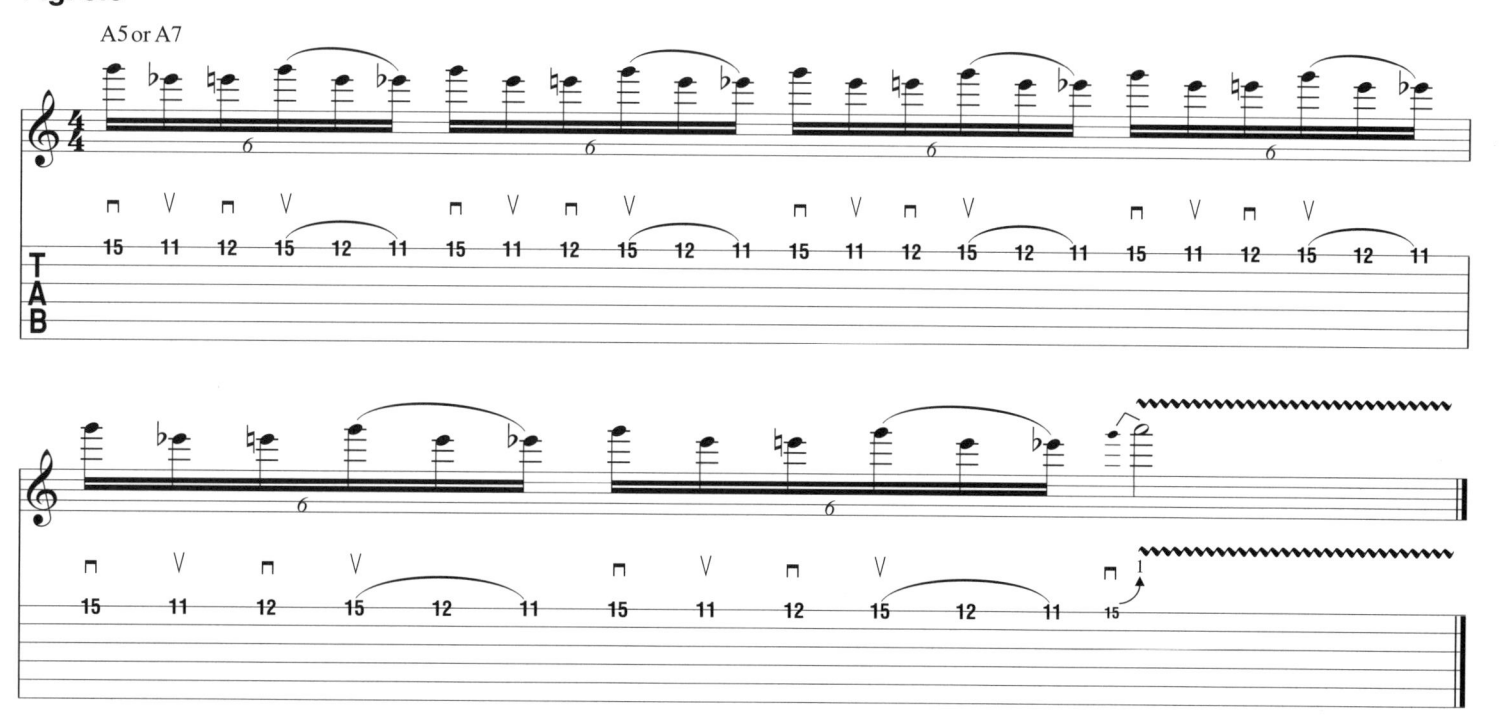

Partial picking can be applied to all of the licks from the previous unit. Keep in mind that experimentation is key to developing you own vocabulary. Here are a few examples to help jump-start your imagination. Figs. 3:10 and 3:11 use the E minor scale (E–F#–G–A–B–C–D) and Fig. 3:12 employs the A minor scale (A–B–C–D–E–F–G).

Track 15
(0:00)

Fig. 3:10

Track 15
(0:08)

Fig. 3:11

Track 15
(0:16)

Fig. 3:12

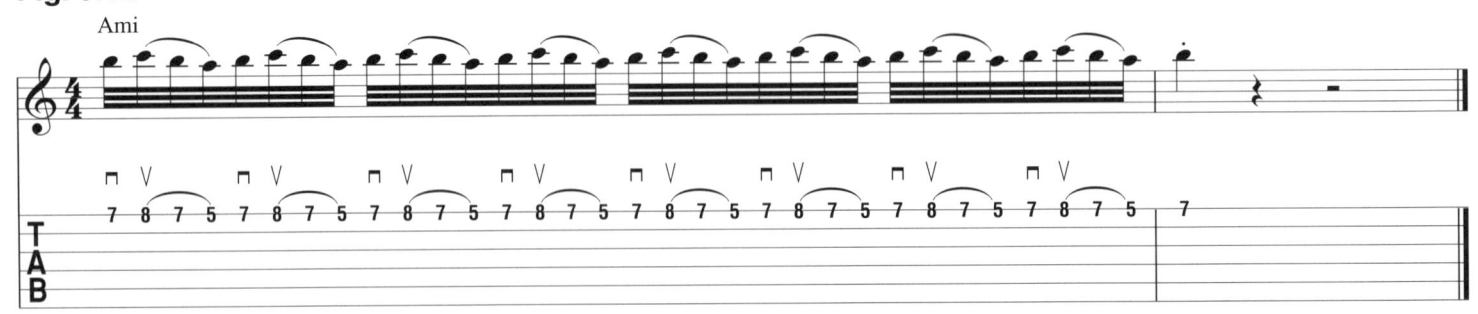

Sweep Picking Part 1

One of the most popular shred techniques is sweep picking. Sweep picking is achieved by raking the pick across the strings using either a continuous downstroke or upstroke. This technique is most commonly used to execute arpeggios with blinding speed and accuracy. The single most important thing to remember when employing sweep-picking techniques is to never sacrifice accuracy and articulation for fast, sloppy, and poorly timed "noise."

Things to keep in mind as you work through this chapter:
1. Practice slowly and perfectly.
2. Don't rush—good rhythm is key.
3. Use left- and right-hand muting to eliminate unwanted string noise.
4. Left-hand fingers should fret notes one at a time—no barre chords! Let the fingers "roll" across the strings evenly and fluently.
5. Pay attention to all pick directions.
6. Be patient. Perfecting sweep picking will take many hours of repetition.

Two-String Sweep Exercises

Fig. 4:1 is a two-string sweep exercise using an A major triad (A–C♯–E). Rake down across the B and high-E strings for the A and C♯ notes, and pick up on the high-E string for the E note. Try not to let the A and C♯ notes ring together. Remember to practice slowly and perfectly (with a metronome) at first. When you can play each example cleanly and in perfect time, speed up the metronome (a little at a time) and practice it at a faster tempo.

Track 16 (0:00)

Fig. 4:1

Fig. 4:2 uses the notes of an Ami triad (A–C–E).

Track 16
(0:04)

Fig. 4:2

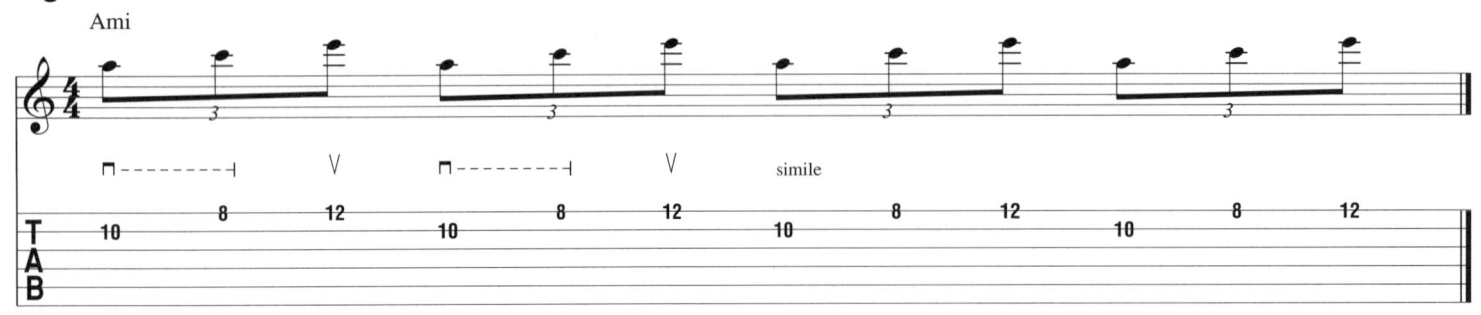

Fig. 4:3 uses the notes of an A° triad (A–C–E♭).

Track 16
(0:09)

Fig. 4:3

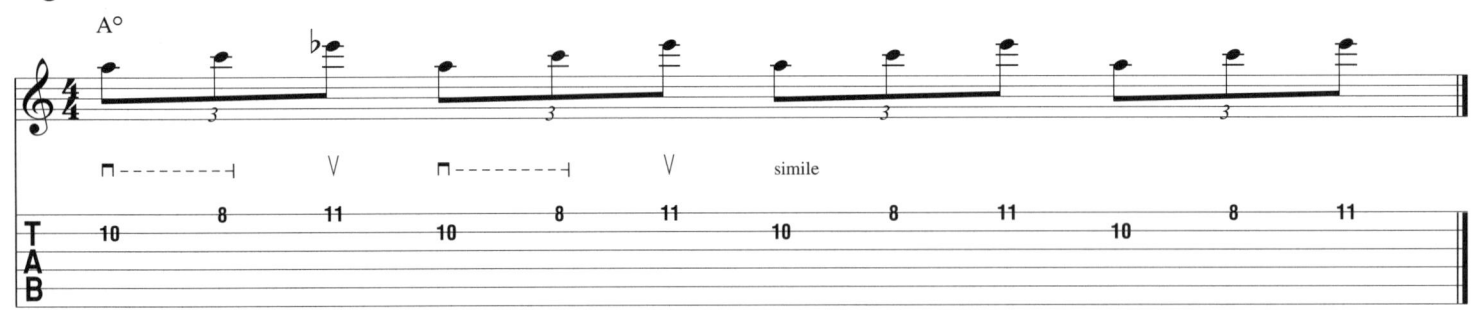

Two-String Sweep Licks

Now let's apply our two-string sweeping technique to a few licks. Fig. 4:4 groups Ami and B° (B–D–F) triads with a partial E7 arpeggio (E–G♯–B–D).

Track 17
(0:00)

Fig. 4:4

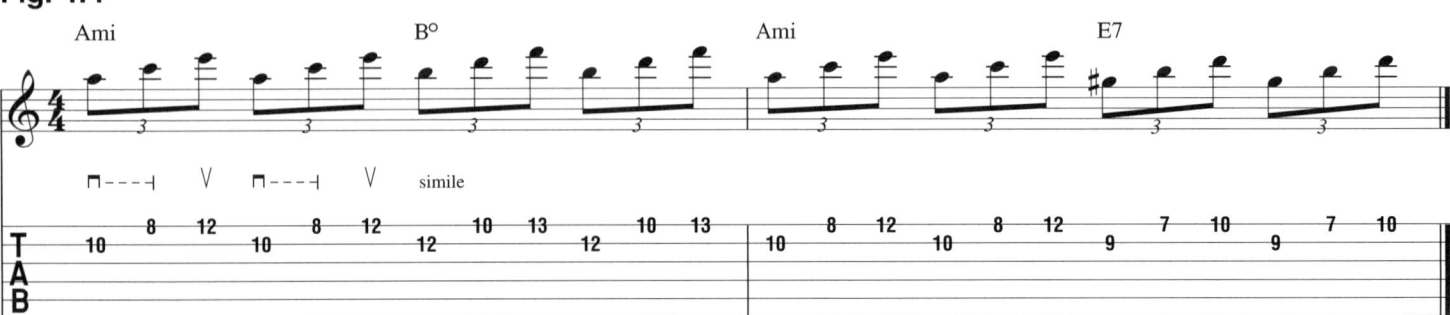

24

Chapter 4

Fig. 4:5 casts several inversions of Gmi (G–B♭–D) and Cmi triads (C–E♭–G), along with a D7 arpeggio (D–F♯–A–C) and an E♭° triad (E♭–F♯–A).

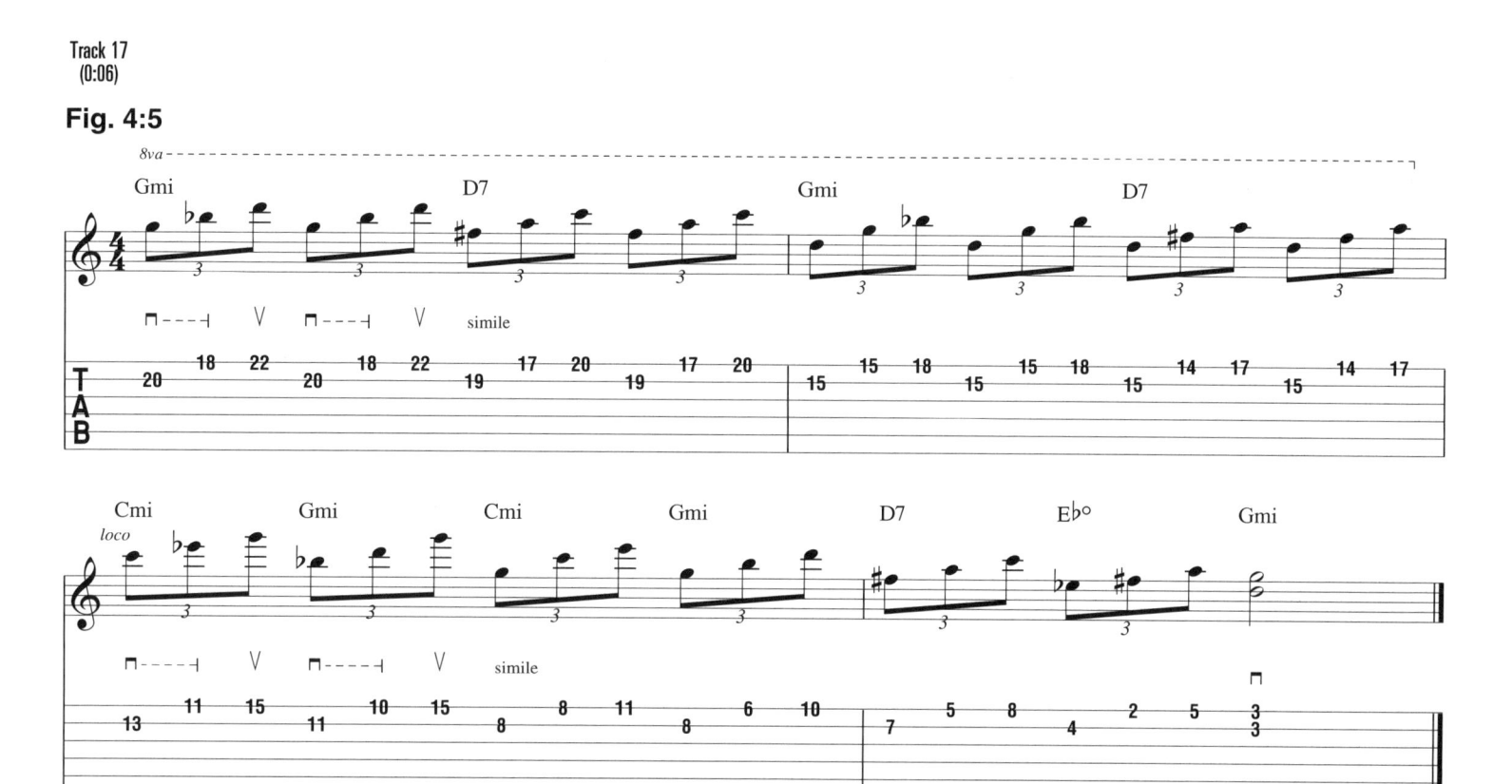

Track 17
(0:06)

Fig. 4:5

Fig. 4:6 throws legato moves into the mix. Ami, A° (A–C–E♭), and Fma7 (F–A–C–E) arpeggios supply the melodic fuel.

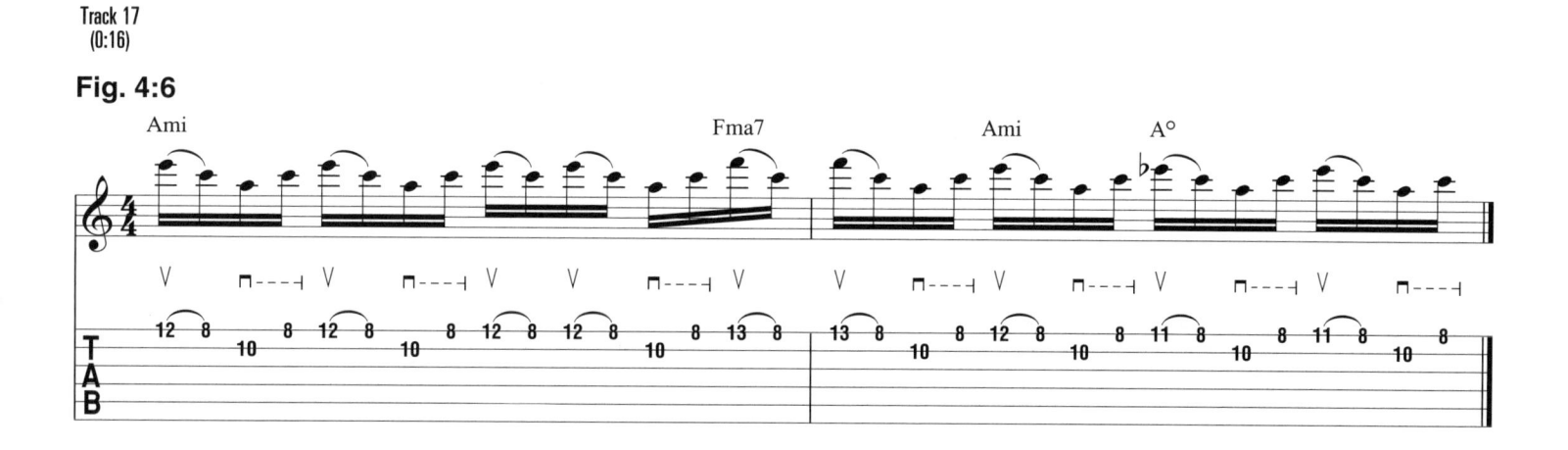

Track 17
(0:16)

Fig. 4:6

Three-String Sweeps

The following exercises apply sweeping techniques to the top-three string set (G/B/high-E). Fig. 4:7 features a one-octave shape of a first-inversion (3rd in the bass) A major triad (A–C#–E). It includes a pull-off legato move, and both down- and upstroke sweeping directions.

Track 18
(0:00)

Fig. 4:7

Fig. 4:8 employs similar sweeping tactics to a second-inversion (5th in the bass) A major triad.

Track 18
(0:05)

Fig. 4:8

Fig. 4:9 features a root-position, A major triad shape.

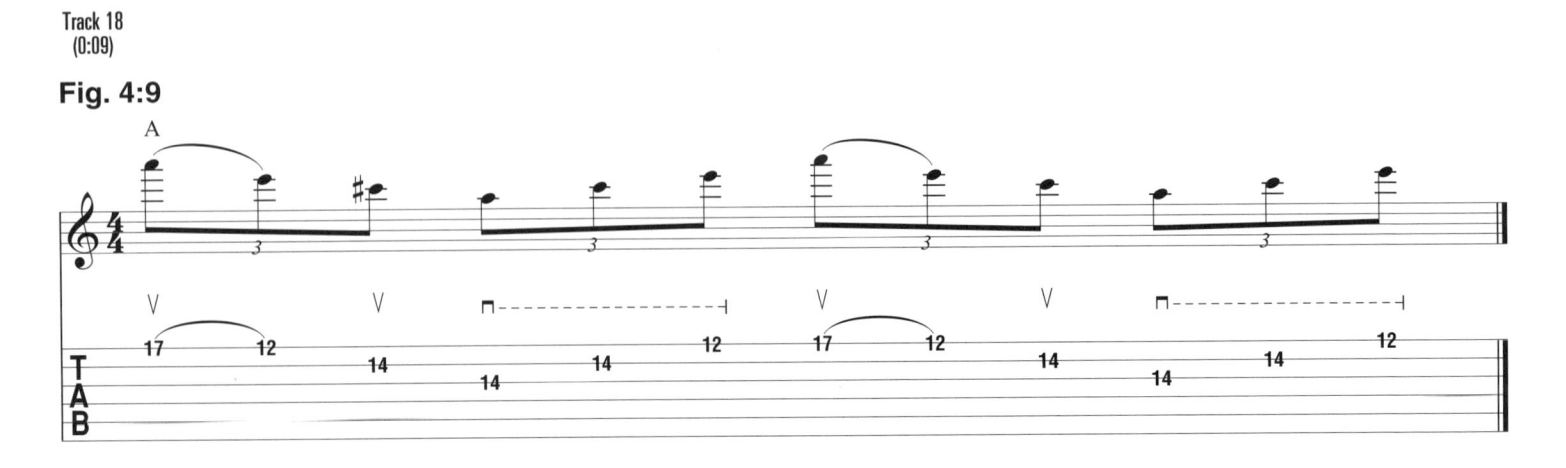

Track 18
(0:09)

Fig. 4:9

Chapter 4

The next three examples apply similar sweeping techniques to inversions of an A minor triad.

Track 19 (0:00)

Fig. 4:10

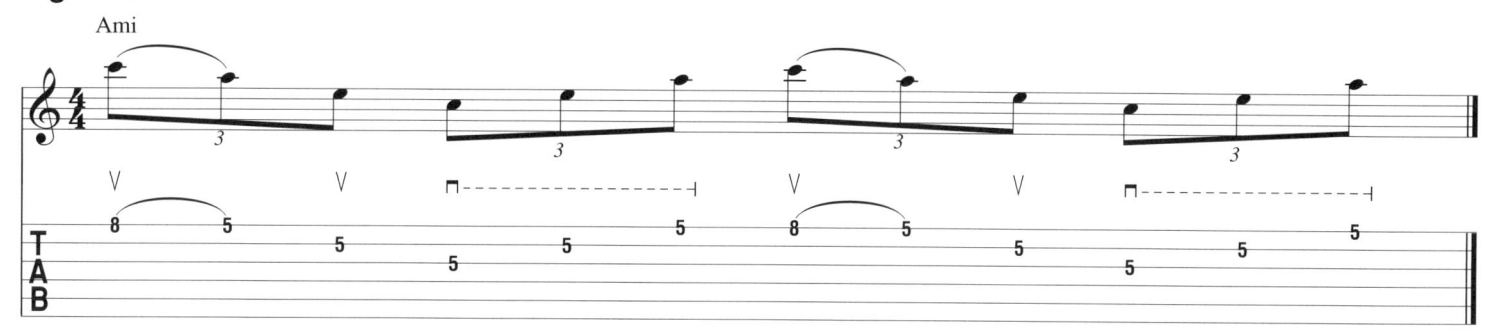

Track 19 (0:04)

Fig. 4:11

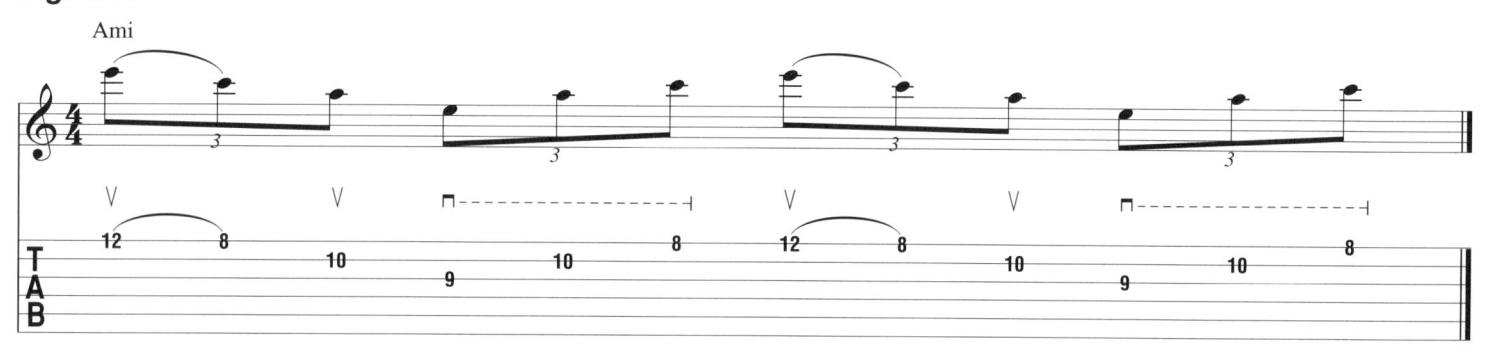

Track 19 (0:09)

Fig. 4:12

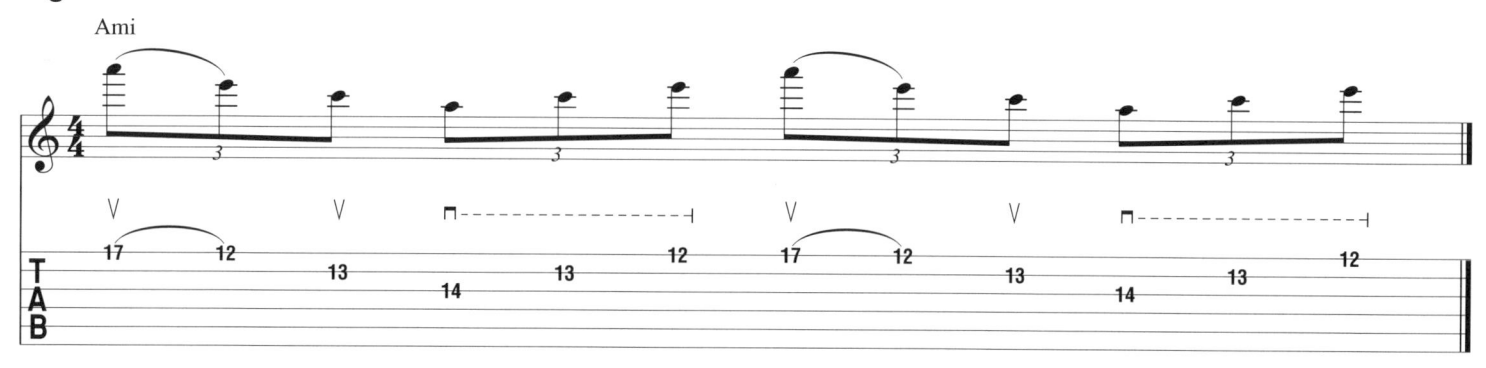

Fig. 4:13 features an A°7 arpeggio (A–C–E♭–G♭). Due to its symmetrical construction (stacked minor-third intervals), this arpeggio can be moved up or down the fretboard in three-fret increments.

Track 19 (0:14)

Fig. 4:13

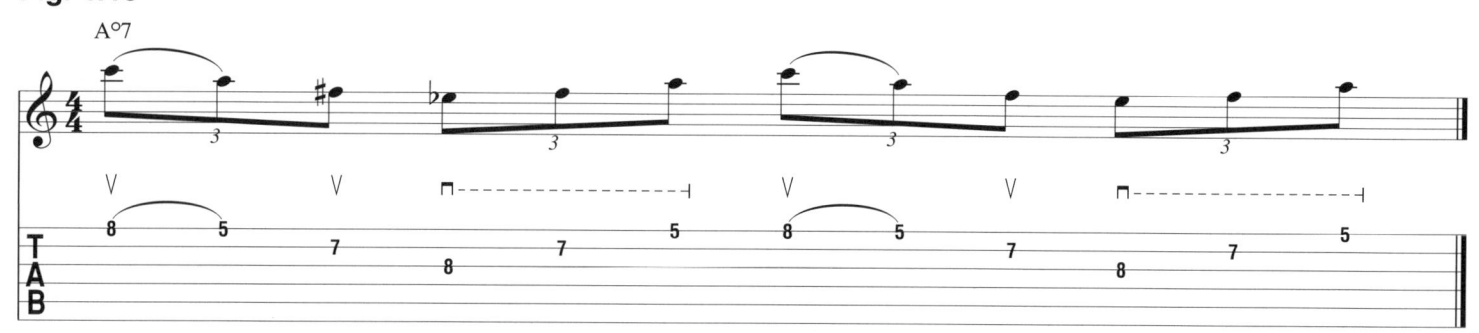

Four-String Sweeps

This next set of examples applies sweeping techniques to the top-four string set (D/G/B/high-E). We begin with a root-position, A major triad. The example starts with a downstroke sweep across all four strings, followed by an upstroke-initiated pull-off on the high-E string, and an upstroke sweep across the B and G strings.

Track 20
(0:00)

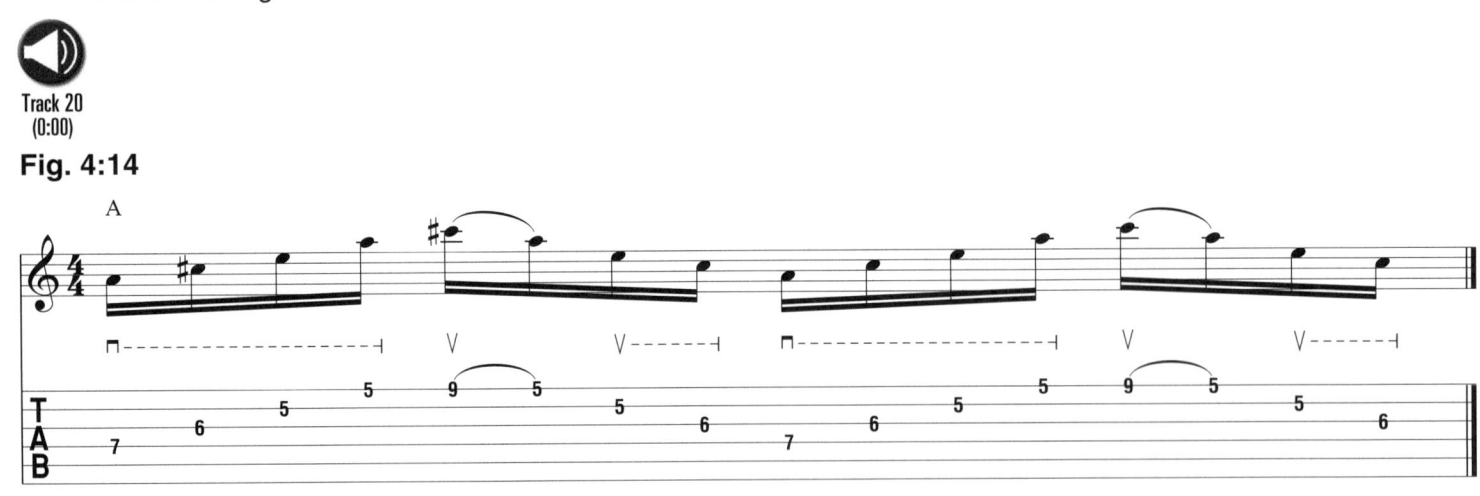

Fig. 4:14

Figs. 4:15 and 4:16 employ the same sweep/legato moves as above, but applied to first-inversion (3rd in the bass) and second-inversion A major triad shapes.

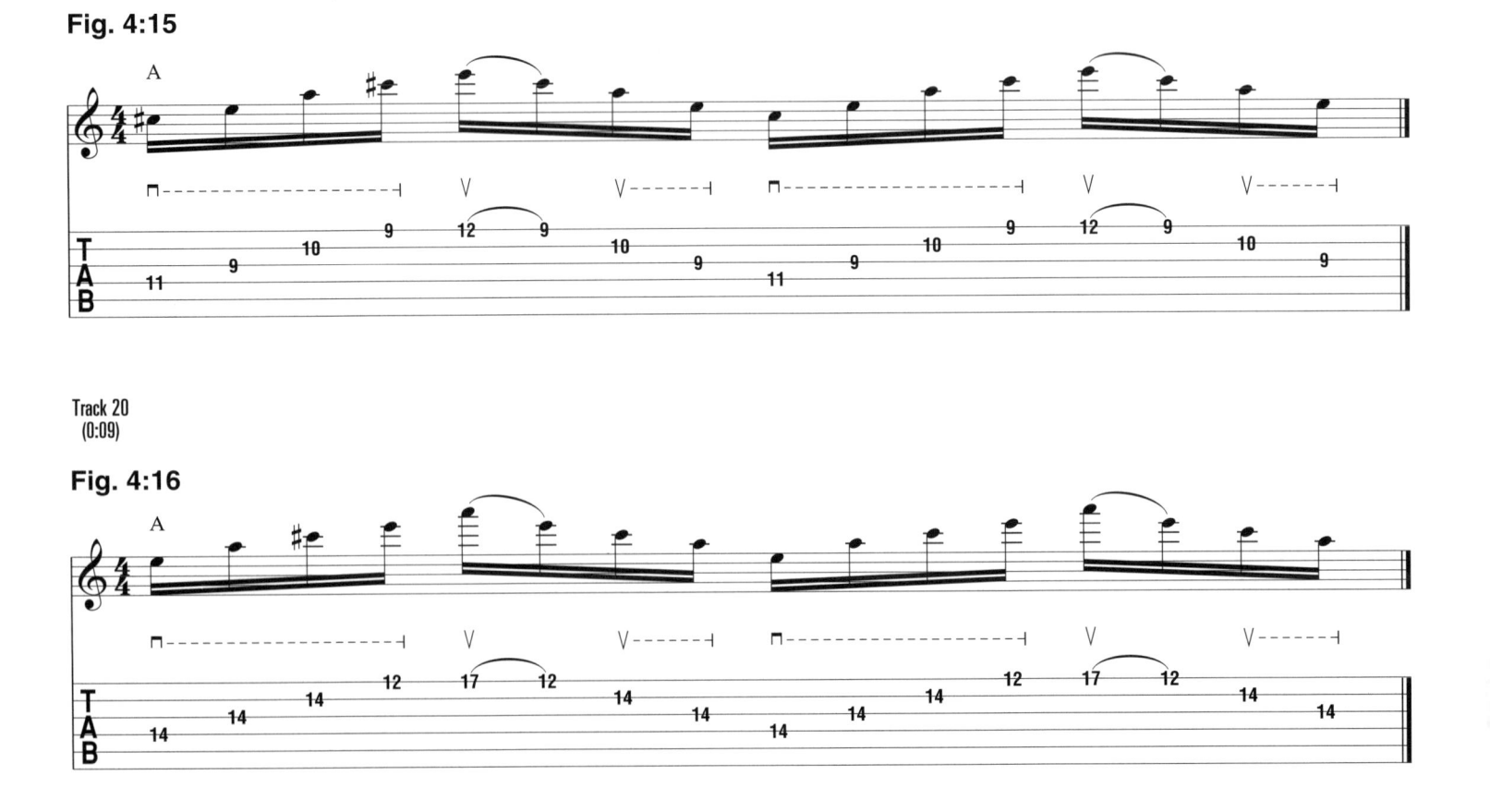

Track 20
(0:04)

Fig. 4:15

Track 20
(0:09)

Fig. 4:16

Chapter 4

The Ami triad examples in Figs. 4:17–4:19 use the same sweep/legato maneuvers as the previous three examples.

Track 21 (0:00)

Fig. 4:17

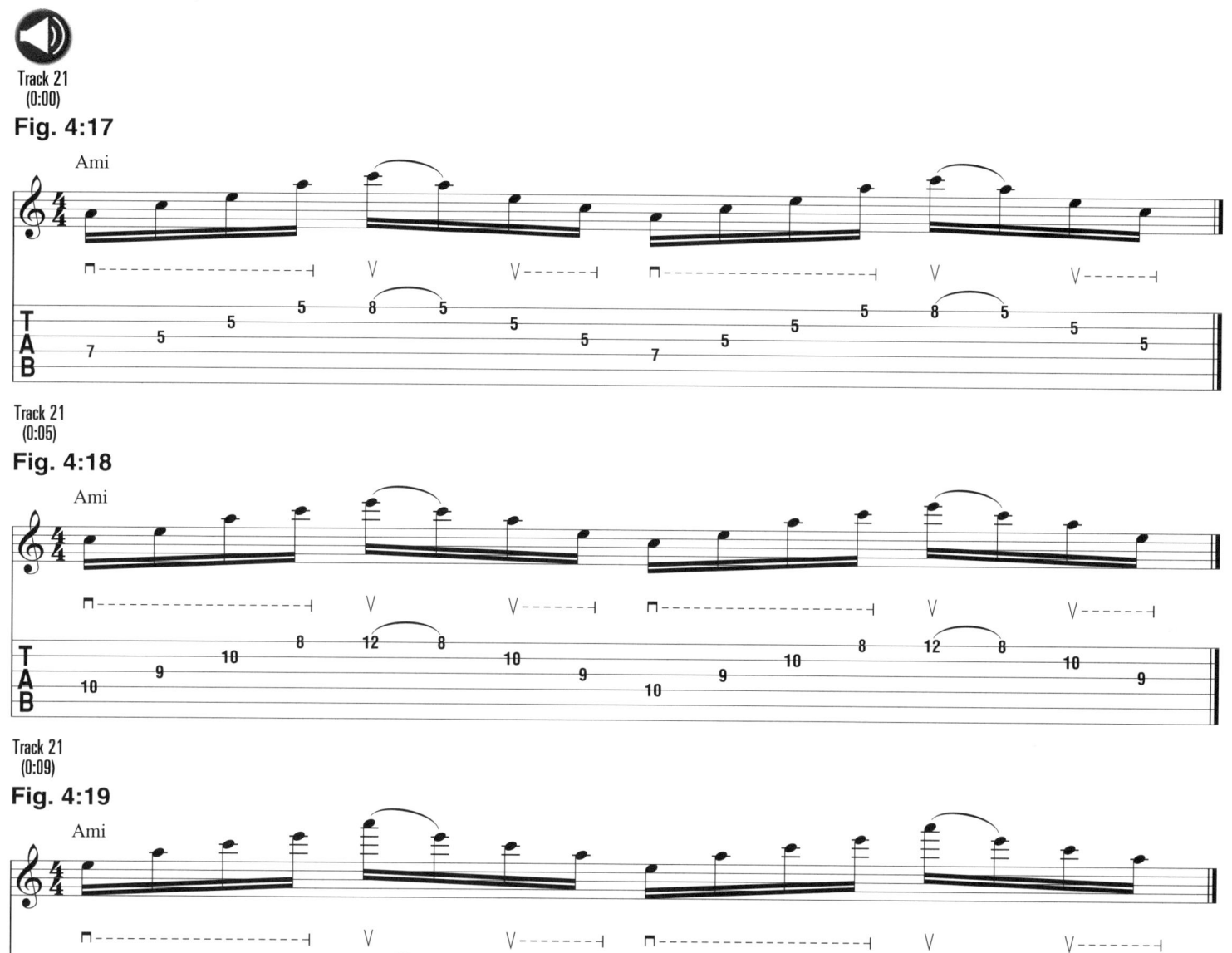

Track 21 (0:05)

Fig. 4:18

Track 21 (0:09)

Fig. 4:19

Fig. 4:20 mixes a variety of hammer-ons, pull-offs, and various sweeps over an A°7 arpeggio (A–C–E♭–G♭[F♯]). Again, due to the symmetrical construction of this arpeggio (stacked minor-third intervals), the lick can be moved up or down the fretboard in three-fret increments. The notation "5" means to rhythmically "squeeze" five notes into the space of four.

Track 22

Fig. 4:20

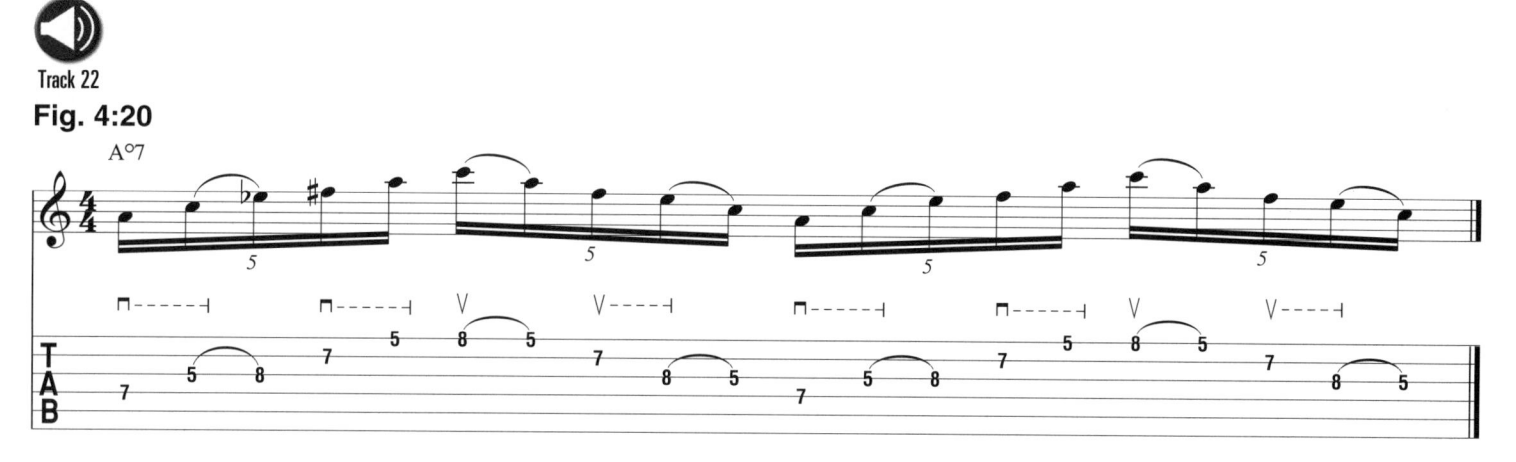

29

Practice all of the previous exercises with the rules we discussed at the beginning of this chapter. When you are comfortable with the exercises, move on to the following etude which combines many of the techniques covered in this chapter.

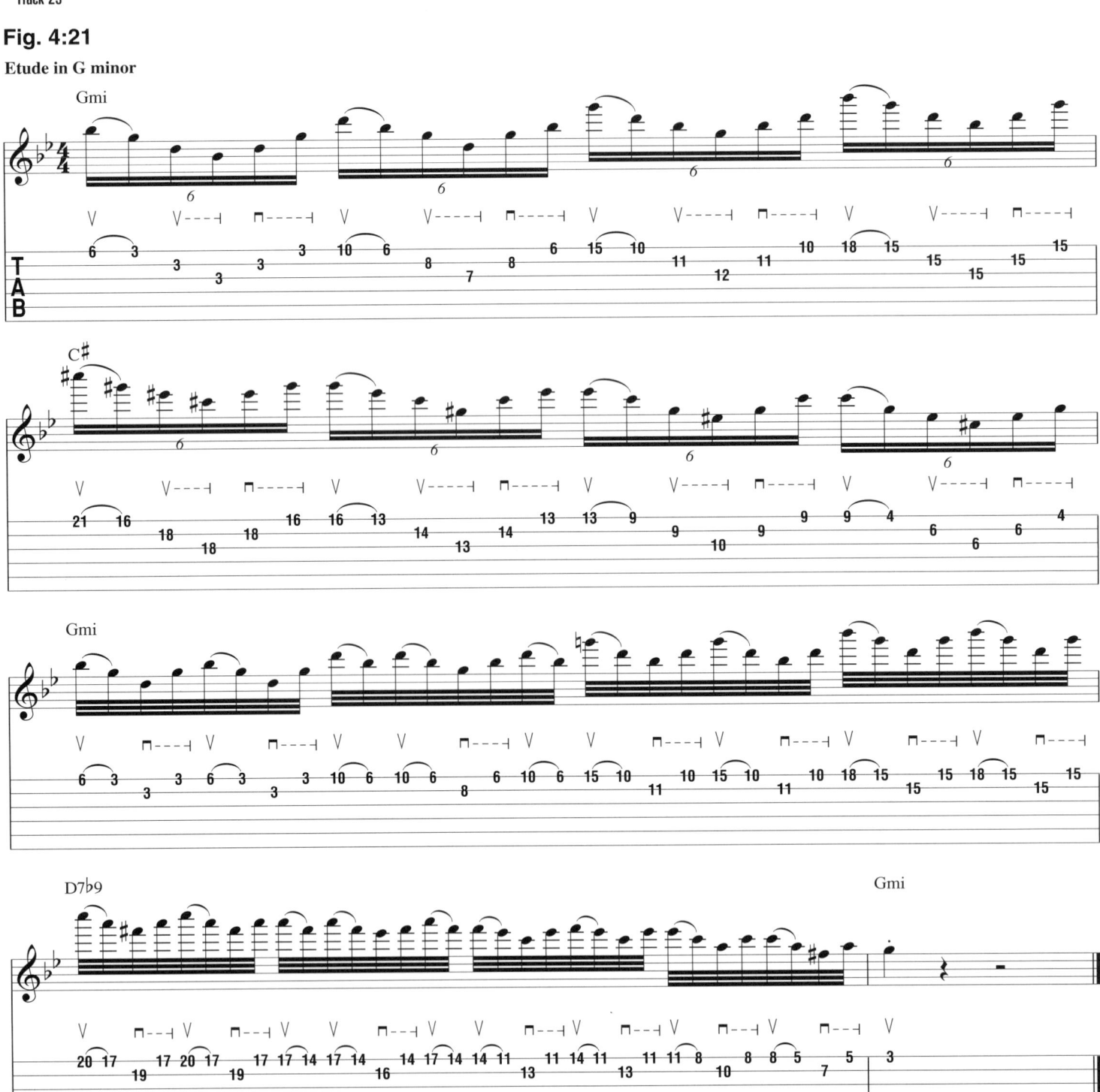

Track 23

Fig. 4:21

Etude in G minor

5

Sweep Picking Part 2

This chapter expands upon the sweep-picking techniques introduced in the last chapter.

Five-String Arpeggio Shapes

We'll begin with some five-string arpeggio shapes. Fig. 5:1 depicts three different inversions of a two-octave, E major triad (E–G#–B). Don't worry about the sweep-picking aspect for now; just get the shapes under your fingers. Due to the wide stretches and position shifts, you'll probably find them particularly challenging. Again, take things slowly, then gradually increase speed.

Track 24

Fig. 5:1

In Fig. 5:2 you'll find the Emi triad (E–G–B) counterparts. Again, don't worry about sweep picking; just memorize the shapes.

Track 25

Fig. 5:2

31

5

Now, let's connect these patterns up and down the fretboard, using sweep-picking techniques. First up is an E major triad example (Fig. 5:3).

Track 26

Fig. 5:3

Emi triad inversions get similar treatment in Fig. 5:4.

Track 27

Fig. 5:4

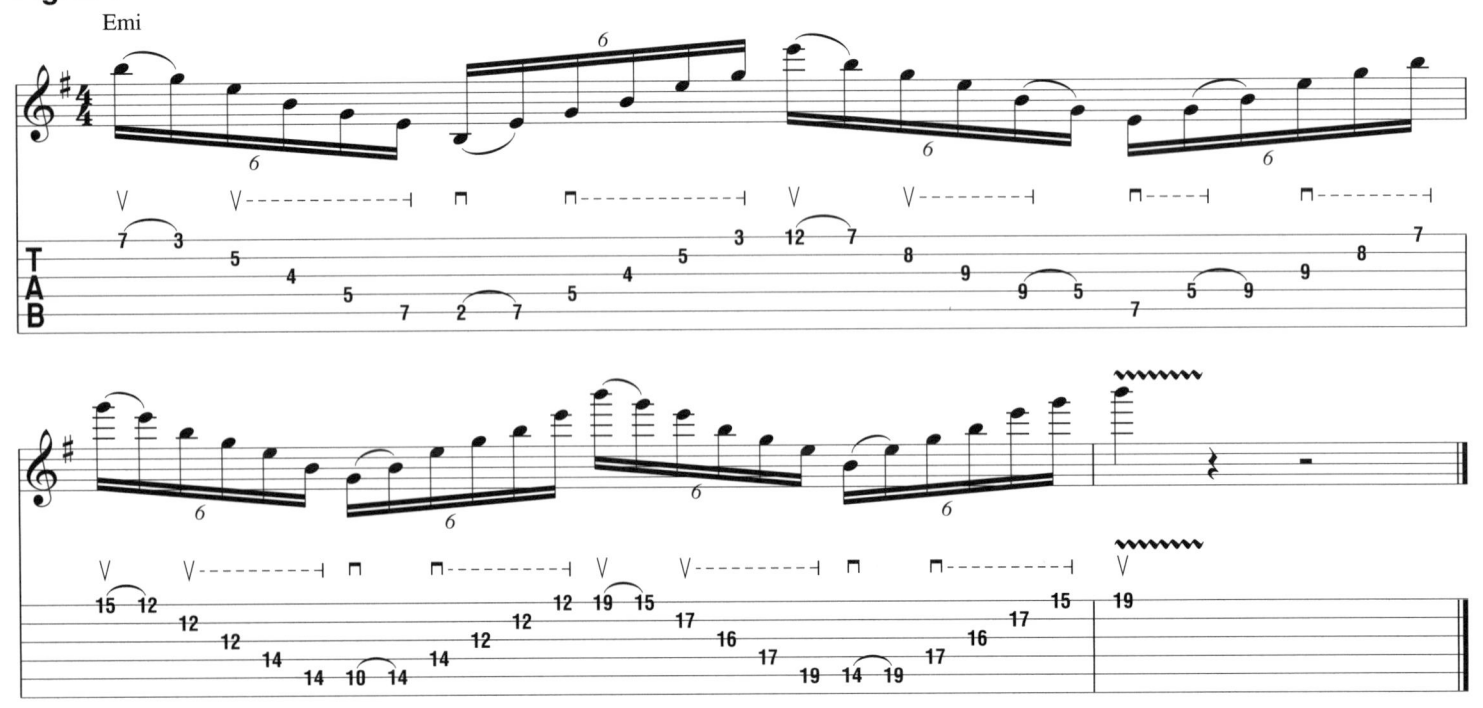

32

Chapter 5

Extended Arpeggio Shapes

Now, let's take a look at a few seventh and extended arpeggios (seventh arpeggios with added notes). Fig. 5:5 recruits a Cma9 arpeggio (C–E–G–B–D) for a sweep-picking lick that involves all six strings.

Track 28 (0:00)

Fig. 5:5

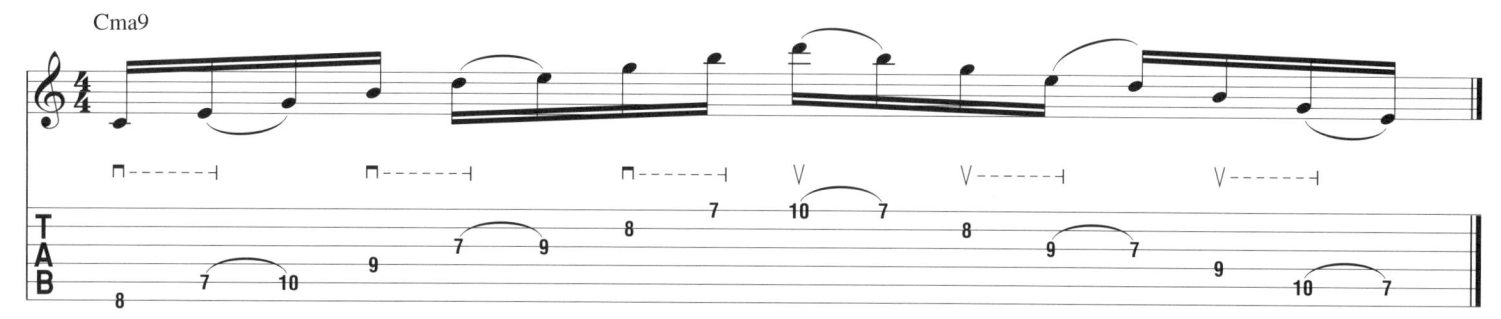

Fig. 5:6 features a different play on a Cma9 arpeggio. By the way, you don't need to wait for a Cma9 chord to come along to dispatch these two licks. They should sound great over most C-major type chords, as well as Ami and Ami7 chords.

Track 28 (0:05)

Fig. 5:6

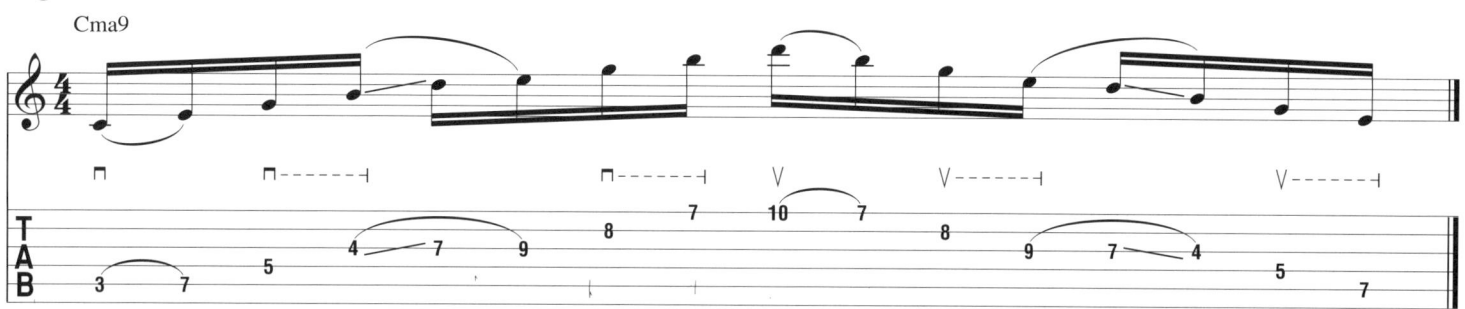

Fig. 5:7 spreads an Ami7 arpeggio (A–C–E–G) across the top five strings. Try using this lick over Ami, C, and Dmi chords.

Track 28 (0:10)

Fig. 5:7

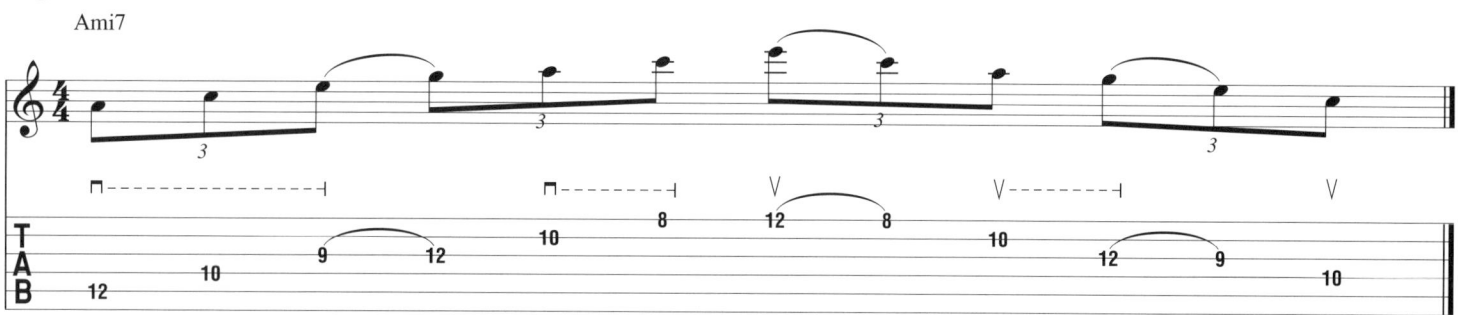

5

Here's a challenging lick (Fig. 5:8) constructed from an Ami11 arpeggio (A–C–E–G–B–D). Try this lick the next time you're soloing in the key of A minor.

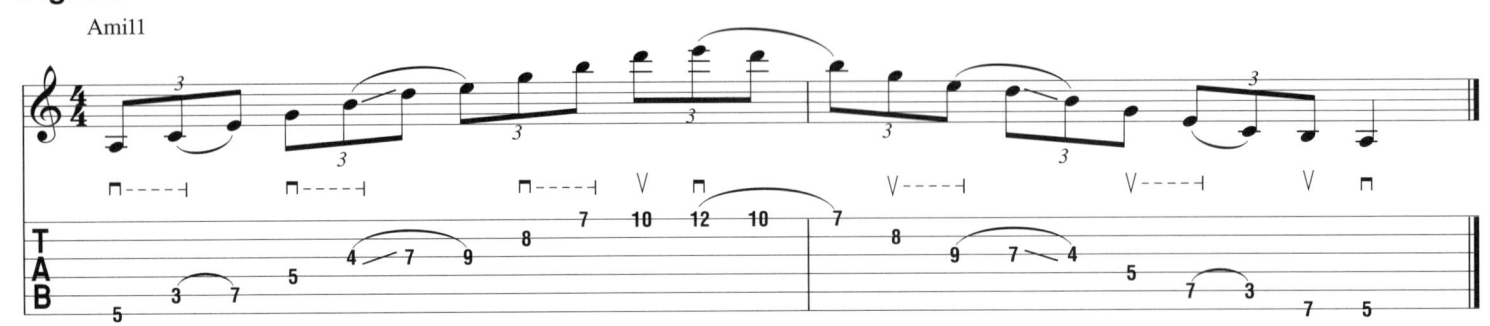

Track 29 (0:00)

Fig. 5:8
Ami11

Hungry for more? Let's check out some four-octave, position-shifting arpeggios that cover all six strings. The first one (Fig. 5:9) is constructed from an Ami triad. Built for speed, it uses all downstroke attacks for the hammer-on ascension, and all upstrokes for the pull-offs on the way back down.

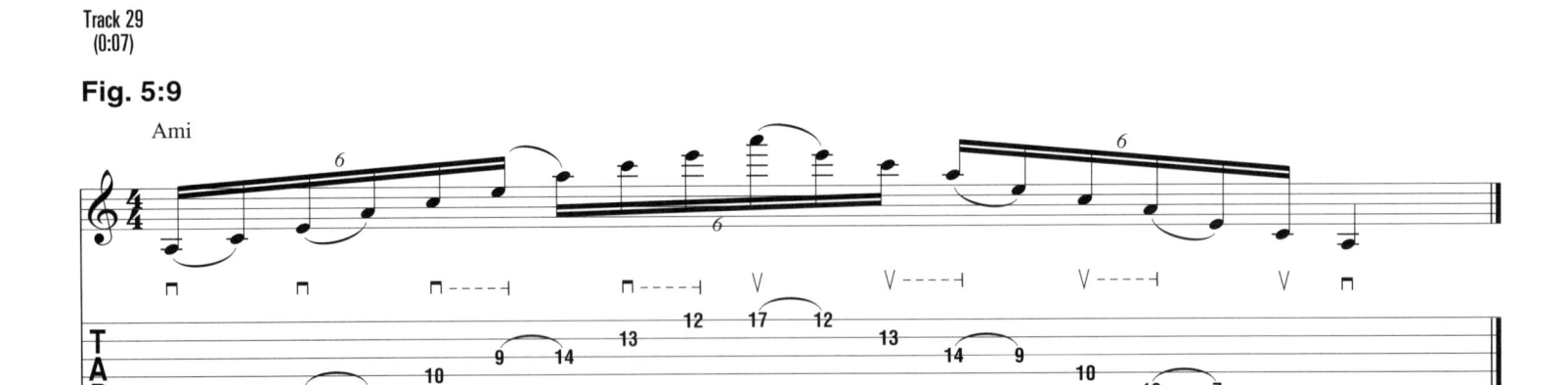

Track 29 (0:07)

Fig. 5:9
Ami

Next up is a C major triad lick. Make sure your timing is impeccable on this one, as it's easy to speed up on the four-string sweeps.

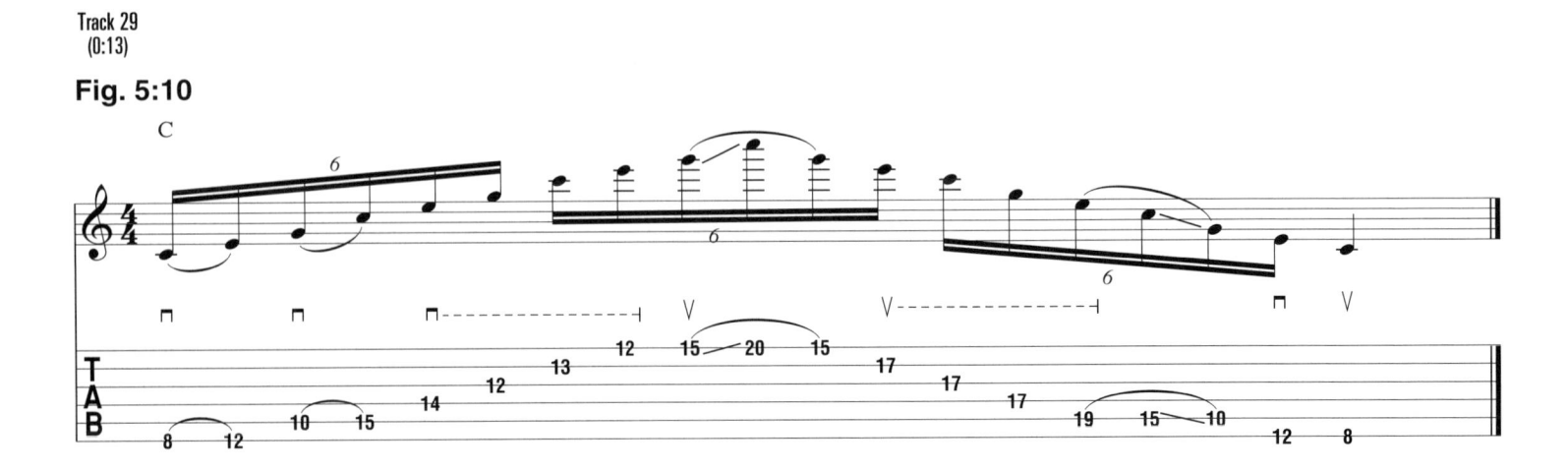

Track 29 (0:13)

Fig. 5:10
C

{{Chapter 5}}

Sweep-Picking Sequences

Here are a few examples of applying sweep-picking tactics to common sequences (Figs. 5:11–5:13). Use them to help kick your creativity into high gear. After you've learned them, experiment with different patterns and various sequences. Add those to your arsenal and write some music!

Track 30 (0:00)

Fig. 5:11
Groups-of-Four Sequence

Track 30 (0:07)

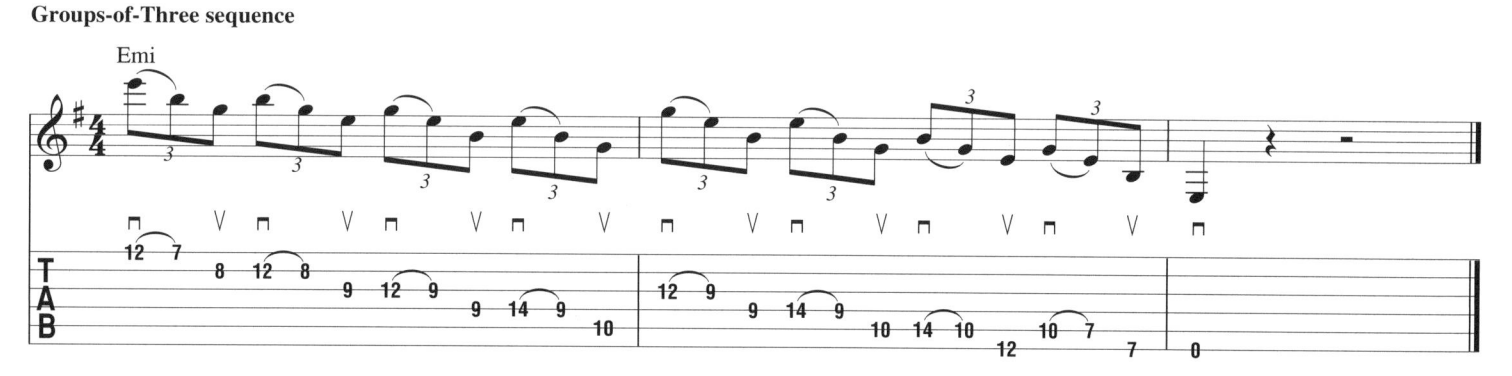

Fig. 5:12
Groups-of-Three sequence

Track 30 (0:15)

Fig. 5:13
Double-Noting Sequence

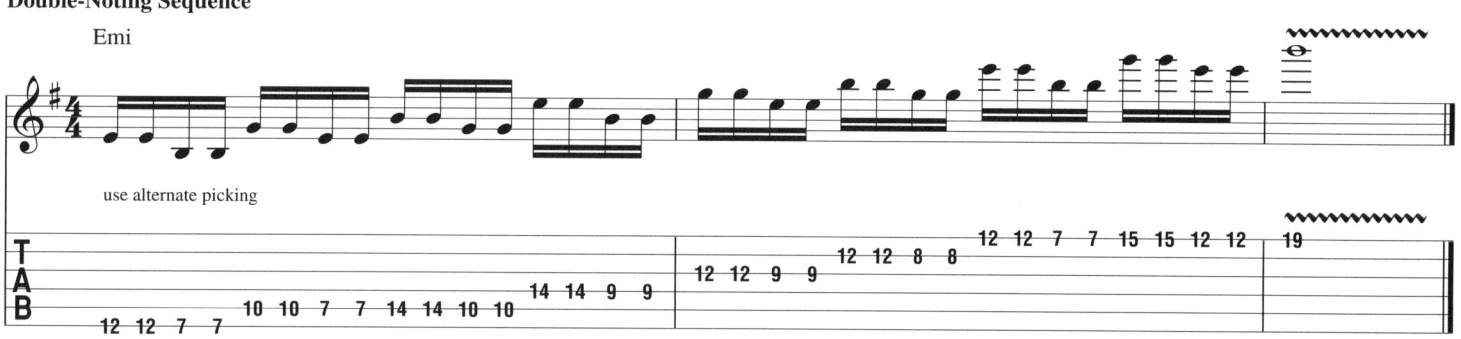

We'll close this chapter with an etude in the key of B minor. It includes an assortment of sweep-picking tactics covered in this and the last chapter. Put it together slowly, measure-by-measure, using the six guidelines outlined at the beginning of Chapter 4.

35

5

Track 31

Fig. 5:14

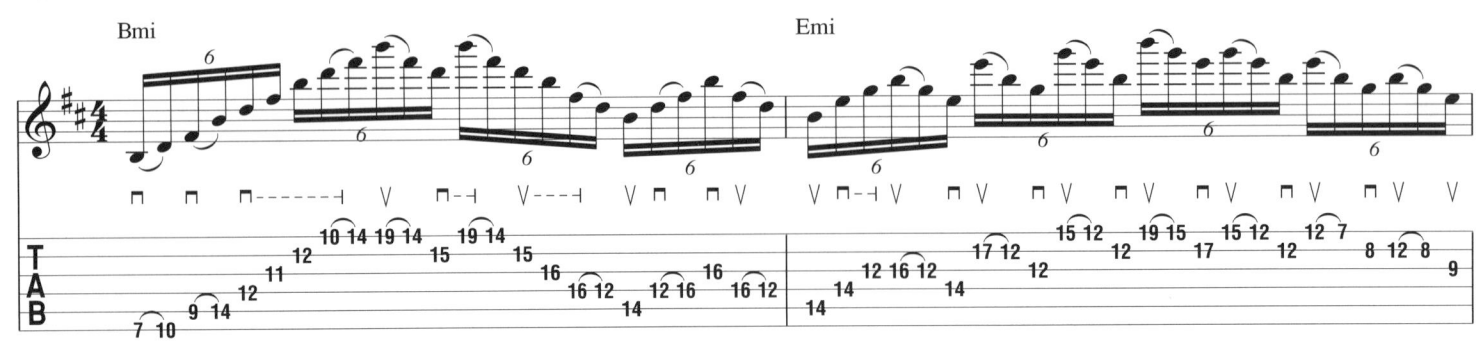

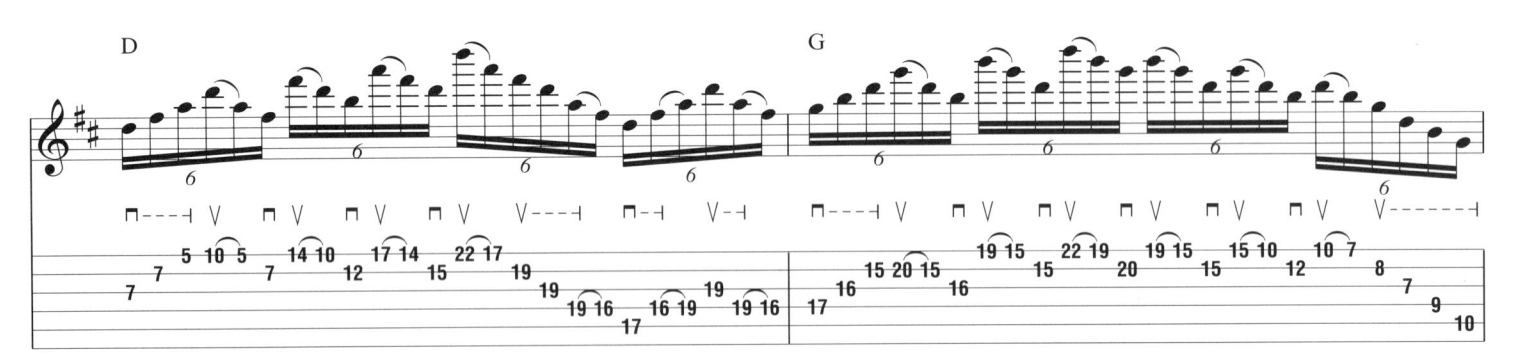

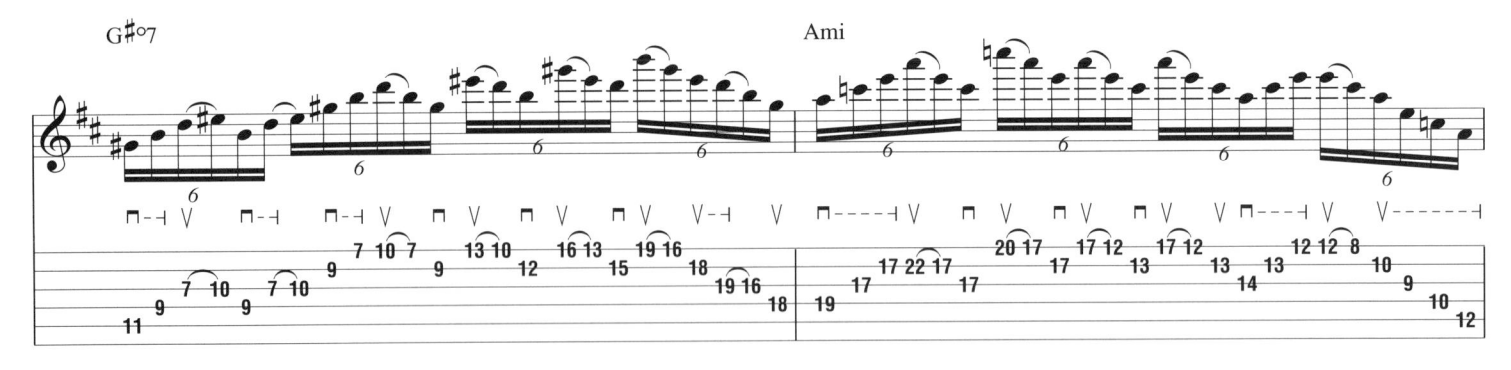

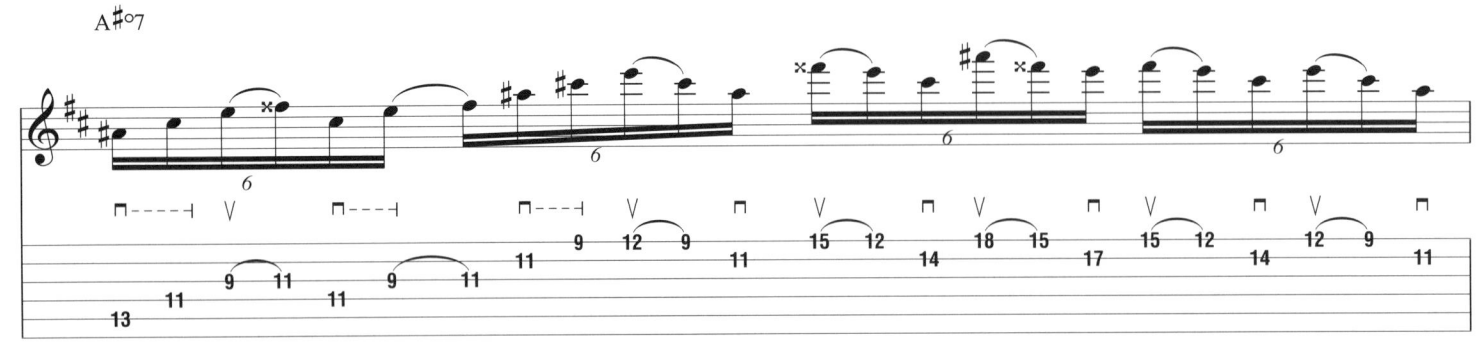

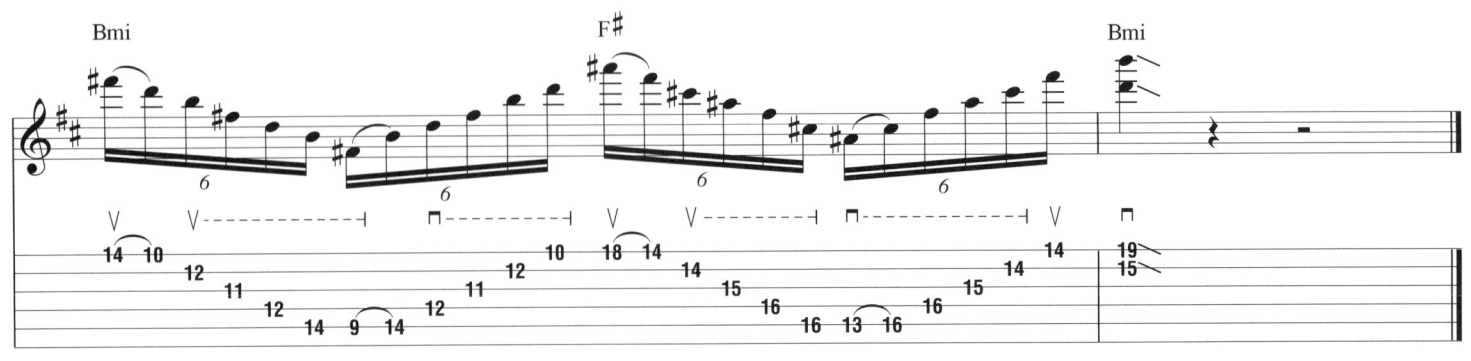

Etude in B minor

Economy Picking

Economy picking is sort of the middle ground between alternate picking and sweep picking, in that it contains elements of each. Look at the two examples in Fig. 6:1 and note the picking directions in each.

Track 32

Fig. 6:1

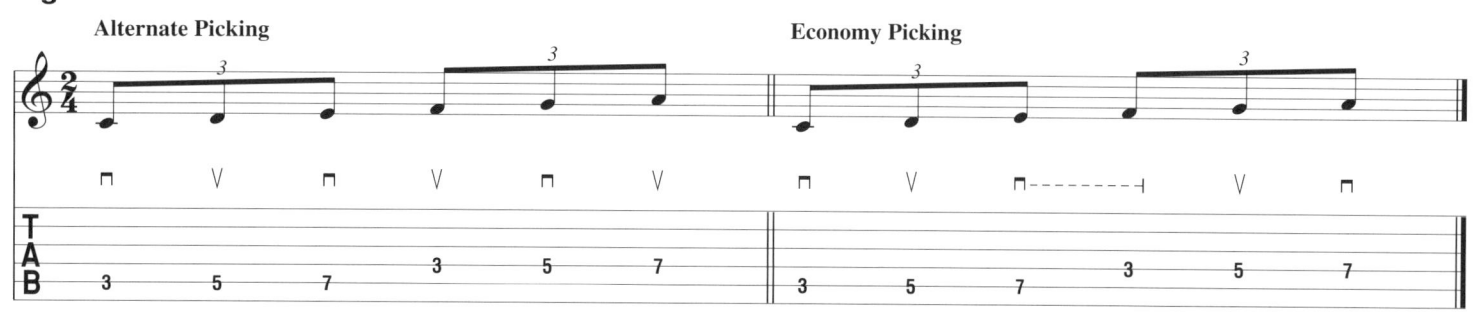

In the alternate picking example, the "down-up-down-up" picking pattern remains consistent. The economy-picking example however, uses alternate picking for the single-string passages, but when the line changes from the A to the D string, a continuous downstroke "sweep" is used.

Economy picking was popularized by Frank Gambale and is a valuable soloing tool—especially when combined with alternate picking and legato techniques. By reducing the amount of pick strokes, it makes it easier to play certain lines and affords greater speed. If this technique is new to you, it may feel a bit strange, but with patience it will pay off—believe me, it's well worth the effort. Here are a few exercises to get you started (Figs. 6:2–6:4). Start very slowly at first, gradually increasing the tempo when you feel comfortable with each example. All three use the G minor scale (G–A–B♭–C–D–E♭–F).

Track 33 (0:00)

Fig. 6:2

6

Track 33
(0:06)

Fig. 6:3

Track 33
(0:12)

Fig. 6:4

This example (Fig. 6:5) combines the previous two exercises and loops them.

Track 34

Fig. 6:5

Here's an example (Fig. 6:6) that uses the relative B♭ major scale (B♭–C–D–E♭–F–G–A).

Track 35

Fig. 6:6

Chapter 6

Economy picking also allows for smooth transitions from arpeggio- to scale-based lines. Fig. 6:7 combines the B♭ major scale with a Dmi7 arpeggio (D–F–A–C) in measure 1, and B♭ (B♭–D–F) and Gmi (G–B♭–D) triads in measure 2.

Track 36

Fig. 6:7

Fig. 6:8 climbs the G harmonic minor scale (G–A–B♭–C–D–E♭–F♯) and culminates with a D7 arpeggio (D–F♯–A–C).

Track 37

Fig. 6:8

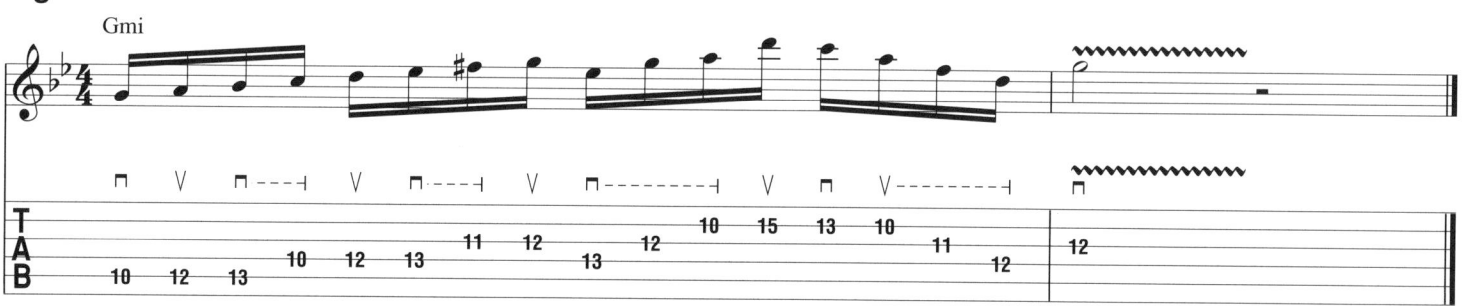

The legato-fueled example in Fig. 6:9 opens with a chromatically enhanced, C major scale line and then moves to a series of seventh arpeggios (D7, G7, G7(♯5), and Cma7).

Track 38

Fig. 6:9

The C major scale example in Fig. 6:10 ups the legato factor with a variety of hammer-ons, pull-offs, and slides.

Track 39

Fig. 6:10

We'll cap off this chapter with a burning lick derived from the E harmonic minor scale (E–F#–G–A–B–C–D#), with curtain-closing Emi triad inversions. It's hard to say which is more difficult: the economy-picking maneuvers or the rhythmic complexity of the lick. [The notation "7" means you are squeezing seven notes (septuplets) into the space of six sixteenth-note triplets (sextuplets).] Put the lick together slowly, beat-by-beat, trying to get the "feel" of the passages as you go. Good luck!

Track 40

Fig. 6:11

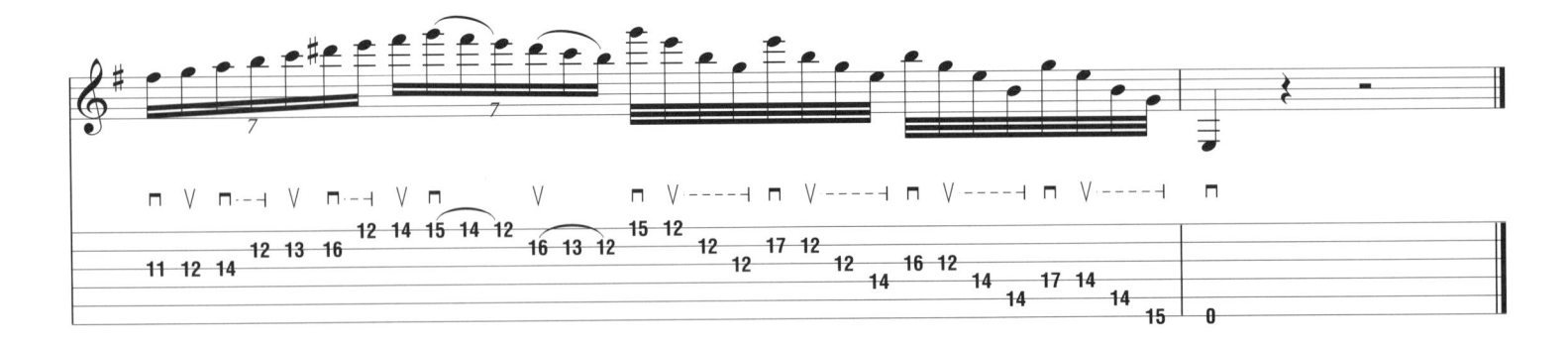

7 String Skipping

In this chapter, we'll take a look at "string skipping" techniques. String skipping can add more color to standard licks by automatically introducing wider intervals. It also offers new incite into the layout of the fretboard, and opens a few more creative doorways. While string skipping is essentially a simple concept, there are a few obstacles to overcome. First, your fret hand has to be extremely accurate and work to mute all unwanted noise. (The picking hand has to "jump" over one or more strings, hindering its ability to mute.) Secondly, your pick hand's movement should be as economical as possible to insure both lightning speed and precision. Keep these things in mind when working through this unit and you'll excel fairly quickly with minimal frustration.

We'll start with a string-skipping exercise that's played exclusively on the G and high-E strings. Using the C major scale as a catalyst, the example starts with a pick/hammer/hammer legato move on the G string, followed by three picked notes on the high-E. The pattern is then reversed, with the legato line (pick/pull/pull) on the high-E string, and the picked notes on the G string; this back-and-forth sequence follows through the entire example. Experiment with different picking directions explained in prior chapters (outside picking, alternate picking, economy picking, etc.) until you find the one that suits you.

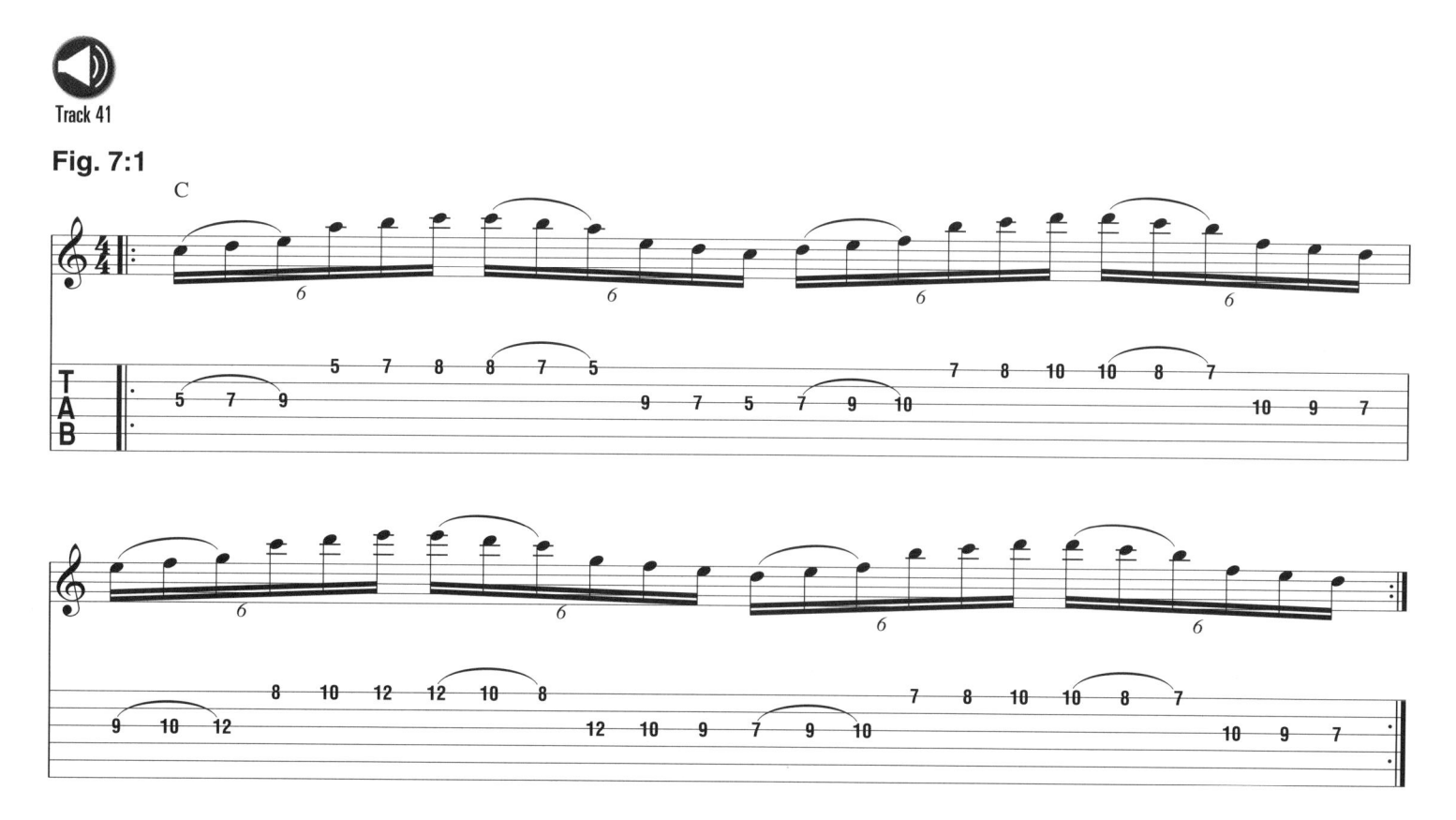

Track 41

Fig. 7:1

Fig. 7:2 expands on the legato/picking pattern from the previous example. Using E Phrygian dominant (E–F–G#–A–B–C–D; fifth mode of A harmonic minor) as the scale source, the example rolls across the fretboard via non-adjacent string sets (low-E/D, A/G, D/B, and G/high-E).

7

Track 42

Fig. 7:2

Here's a G minor scale (G–A–B♭–C–D–E♭–F) string-skipping lick that's just dripping with legato moves (Fig. 7:3).

Track 43

Fig. 7:3

Fig. 7:4 applies string-skipping tactics to the A blues scale (A–C–D–E♭–E–G). You may find that a combination of sweep picking and outside picking works best for this one.

Track 44

Fig. 7:4

Chapter 7

Fig. 7:5 pushes the shred envelope with a trio of bookmatched legato motifs that climb three octaves of the A blues scale.

Track 45

Fig. 7:5

Here's a finger-friendly, A minor pentatonic (A–C–D–E–G) example (Fig. 7:6).

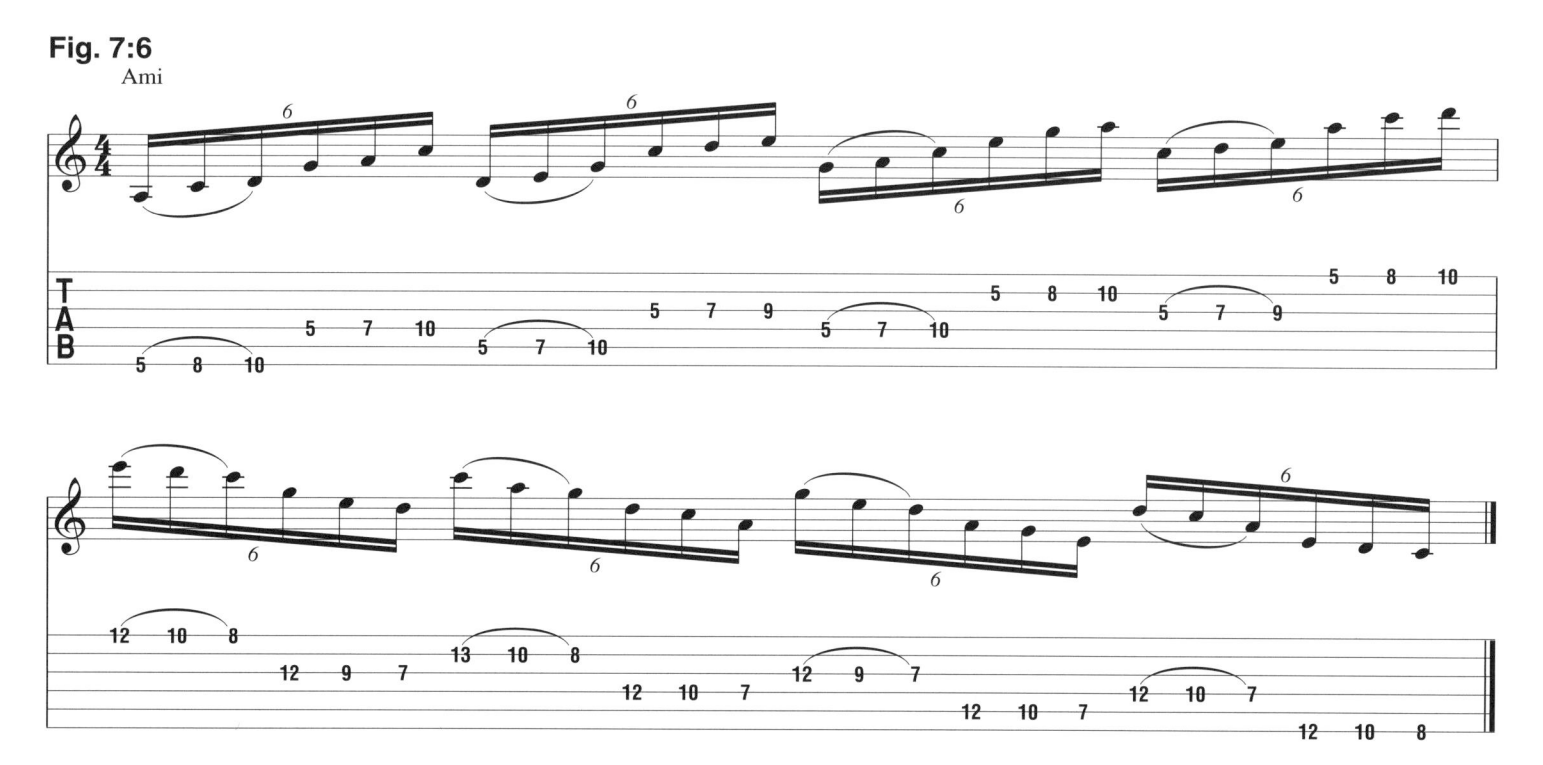

Track 46

Fig. 7:6

String skipping is also a great way to sequence arpeggios. The next few examples demonstrate this procedure in the style of Paul Gilbert. Fig. 7:7 mates a C major triad (C–E–G) with a B° triad (B–D–F). Again, feel free to experiment with different picking directions.

43

7

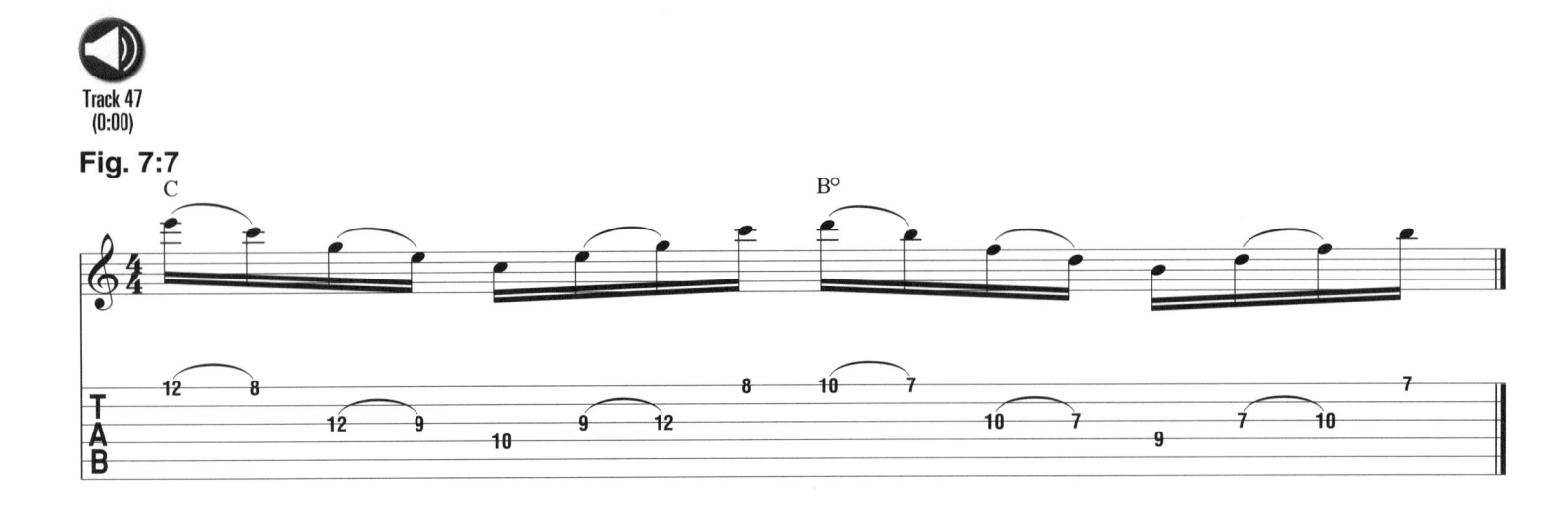

Track 47
(0:00)

Fig. 7:7

Track 47
(0:06)

Fig. 7:8 juggles an Emi triad (E–G–B) with D#°7 arpeggios (D#–F#–A–C) over a I–V7♭9 (Emi–B7♭9) progression in the key of E minor.

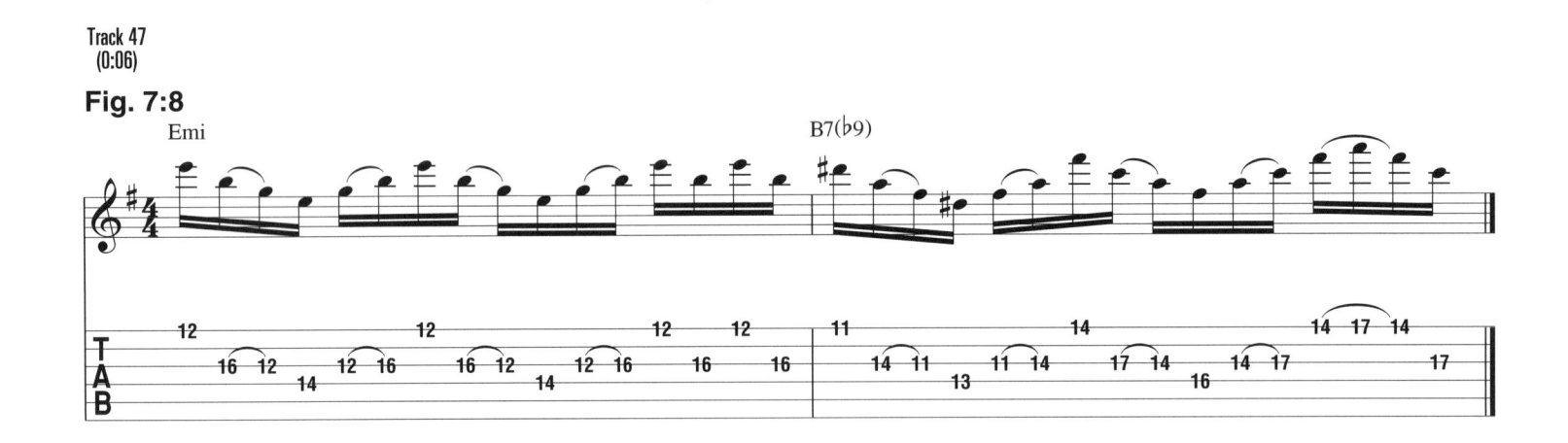

Fig. 7:8

Taking this idea a bit further, let's combine some scale and arpeggio ideas for even more devastating licks. Fig. 7:9 combines C major triad inversions with C major scale passages.

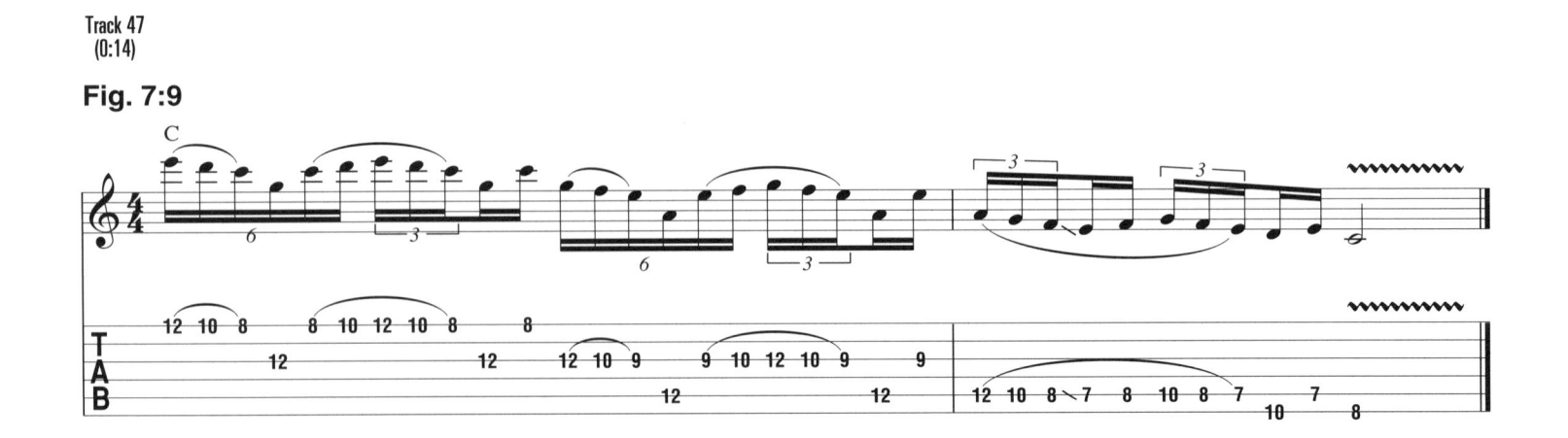

Track 47
(0:14)

Fig. 7:9

Chapter 7

Fig. 7:10 is an extended variation on the previous example.

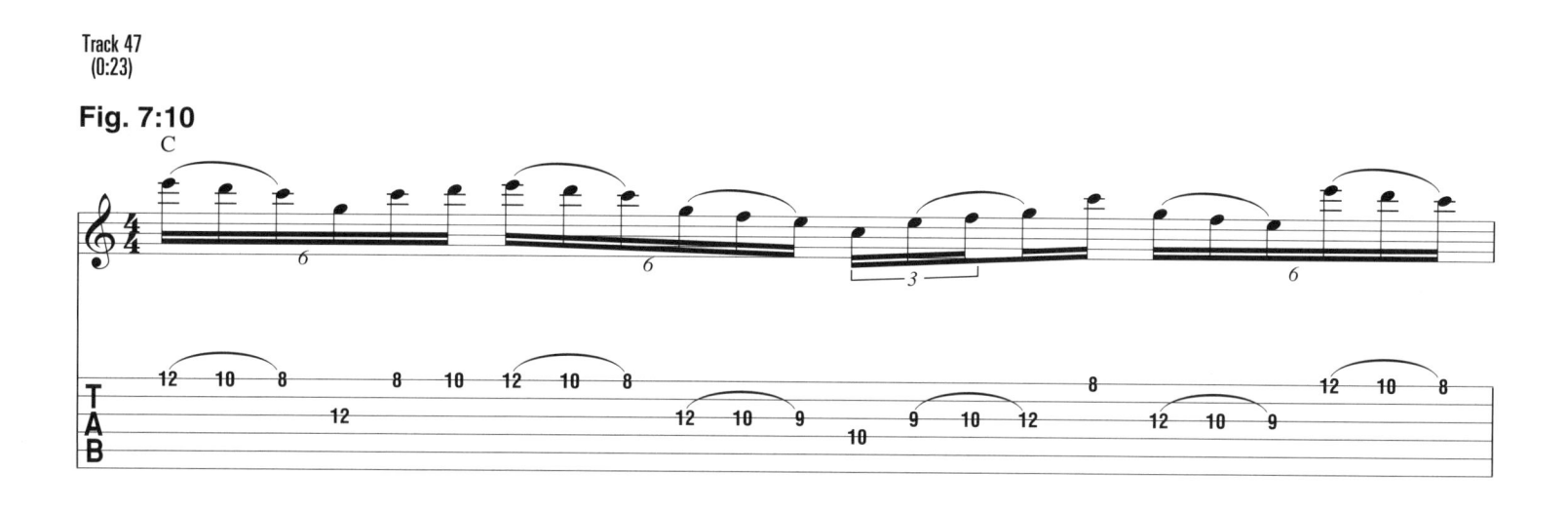

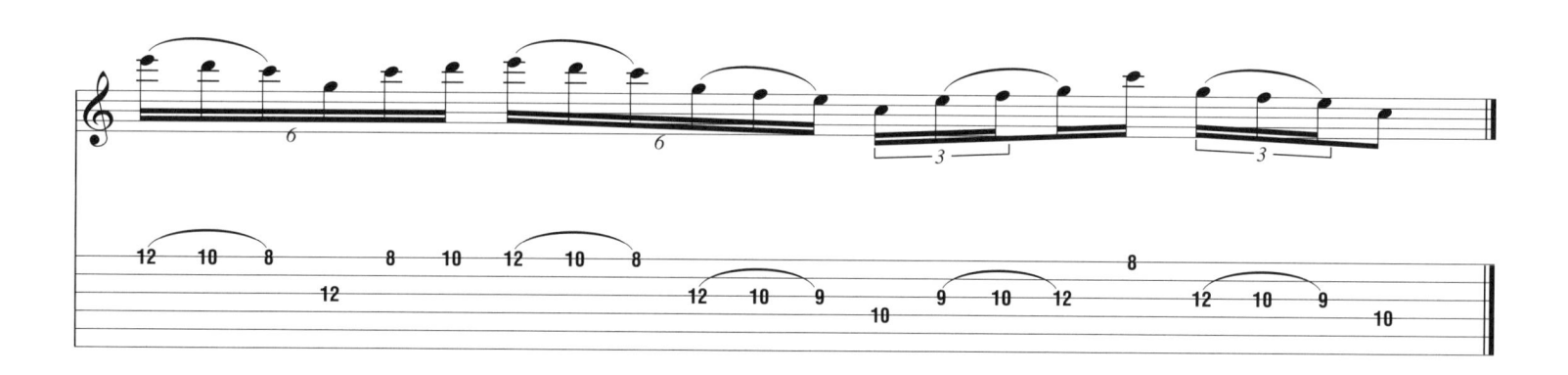

Track 47
(0:23)

Fig. 7:10

We'll close out this chapter with an etude based in the key of A minor. Stuffed with string-skipping passages, it's constructed with a series of extended arpeggios: Ami9 (A–C–E–G–B) in measure 1, Dmi(add9) (D–F–A–E) in measure 2, B°7 (B–D–F–Ab) in measure 3, Cma7(#11) (C–E–G–B–F#) in measure 4, Fmaj9(#11) (F–A–C–E–G–B) in measure 5, Bb13(b9) (Bb–D–F–Ab–Cb–G) in measure 6, Ami7 (A–C–E–G) in measure 7, and E7(b9) (E–G#–B–D–F) in measure 8. Go slowly, putting the etude together bar-by-bar, then practice it in its entirety (also at a slow tempo) for continuity. When you can play it perfectly at a medium tempo, start increasing the metronome setting until you can perform it at a shred tempo.

7

Track 48

Fig. 7:11

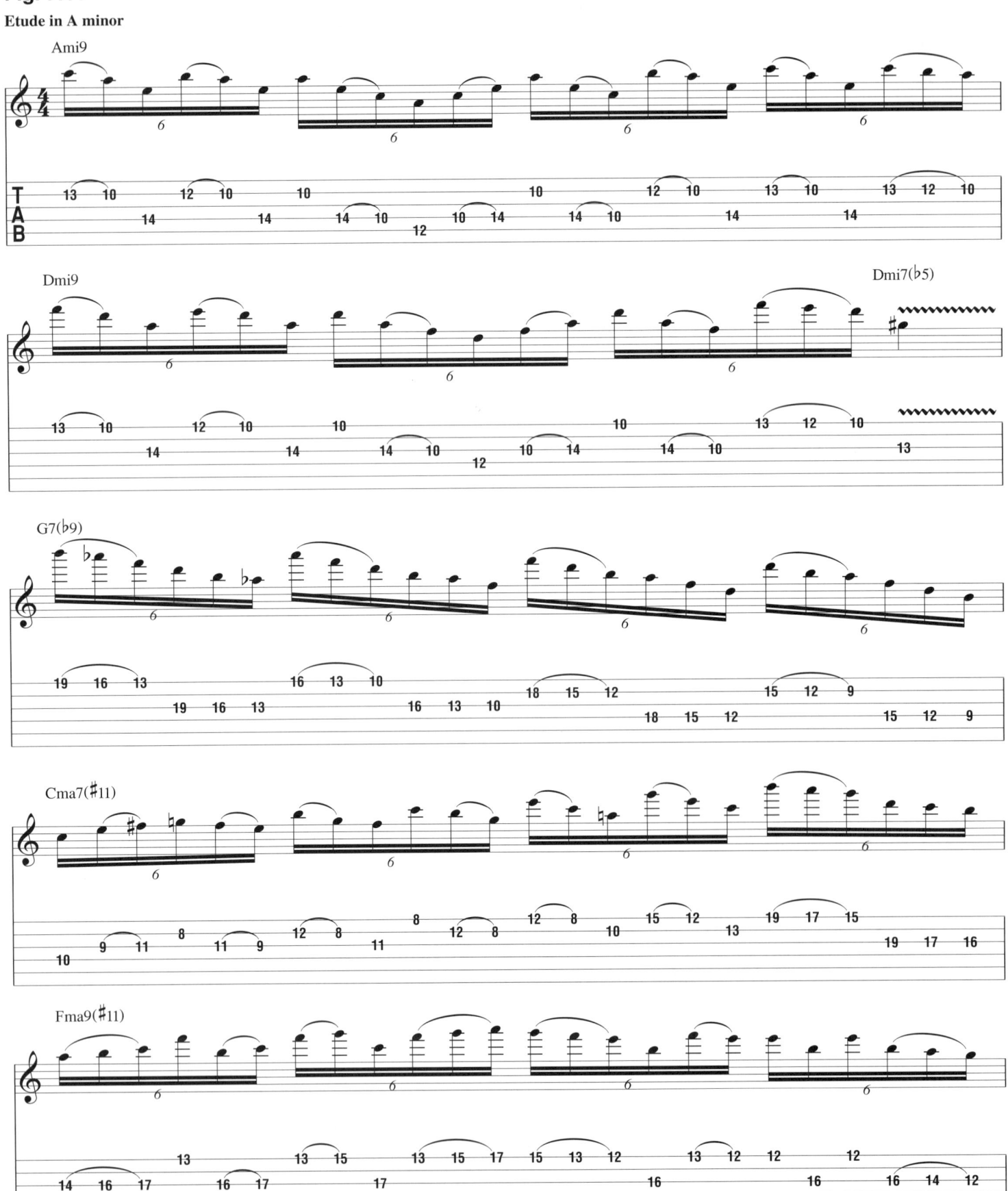

Etude in A minor

Chapter 7

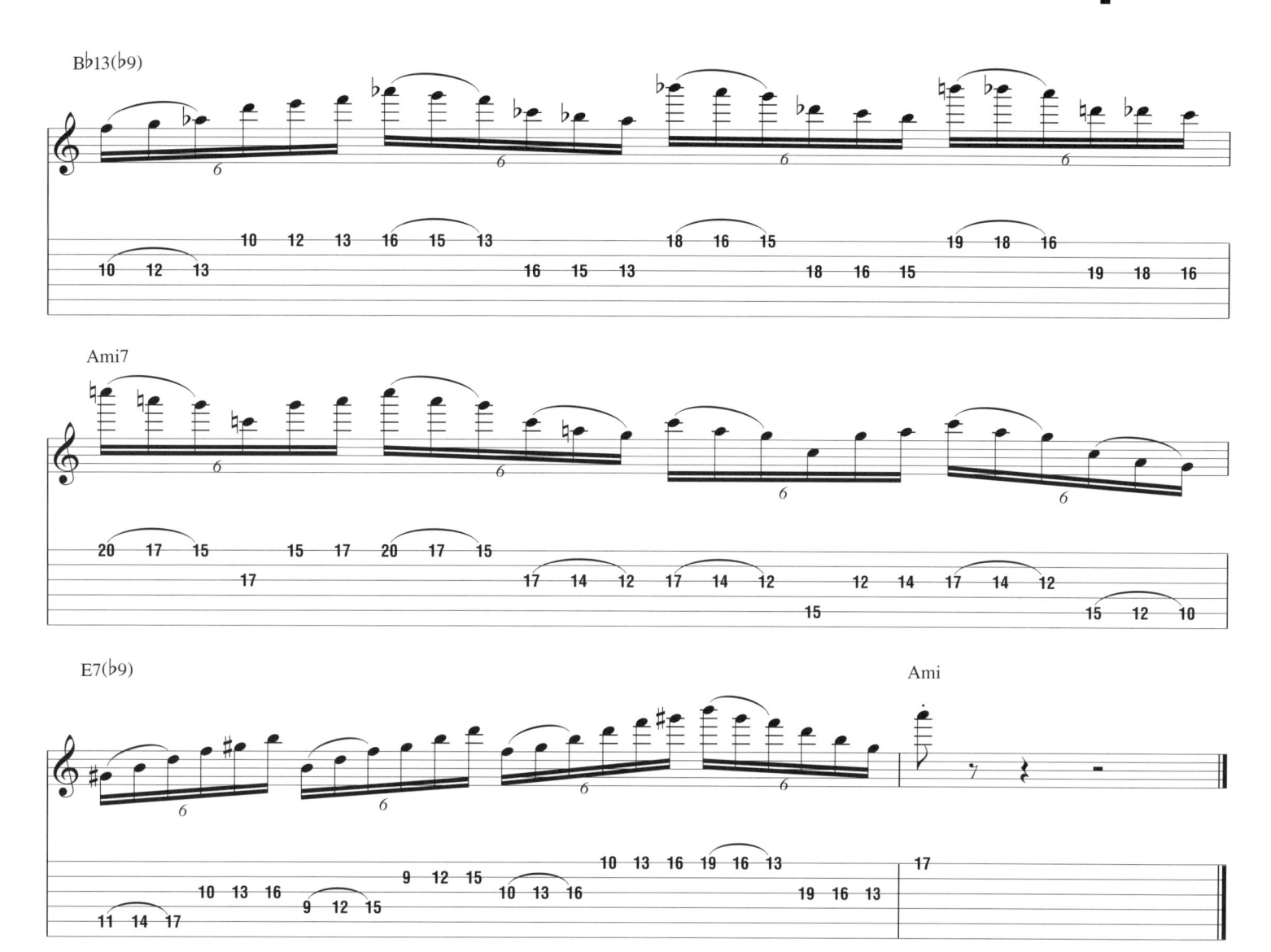

Tapping
8

Few techniques are as essential to shred guitar as tapping (hammering on to notes on the fretboard with the pick-hand fingers). Without it, Eddie Van Halen's "Eruption" would hardly be regarded as an innovation in hard rock guitar. Many players have adopted the tapping technique because of the fluidity it brings to the table.

When using the tapping technique, proper muting is absolutely essential. When your picking hand reaches to the fretboard, make sure your palm comes in contact with all unused strings. Also, some players tap with their first finger while others prefer the middle finger—it's all about what works for you. Hey, we'll even take a look at using all four fingers!

We'll start the ball rolling with a few symmetrical tapping licks in the style of Eddie Van Halen. The first one (Fig. 8:1) is a chromatically enhanced, A Dorian (A–B–C–D–E–F#–G; second mode of G major) example. Start by tapping down on the 12th fret (the same area where you would normally fret that note with your fret-hand finger) of the high-E string with your index or middle finger. Then, quickly remove that finger from the fretboard using either a downward or upward "flicking" motion. (Essentially, this should produce the same sound as a fret-hand pull-off technique.) Your fret hand index finger should already be fretting the 5th fret of the high-E string, so your "tap" will have a note to release to. From there, perform the hammer-ons to the 7th and 8th frets. Then, tap the string again at the 12th fret again and pull-off to the 8th, 7th, and 5th frets. The remainder of the example is played in similar fashion on different strings.

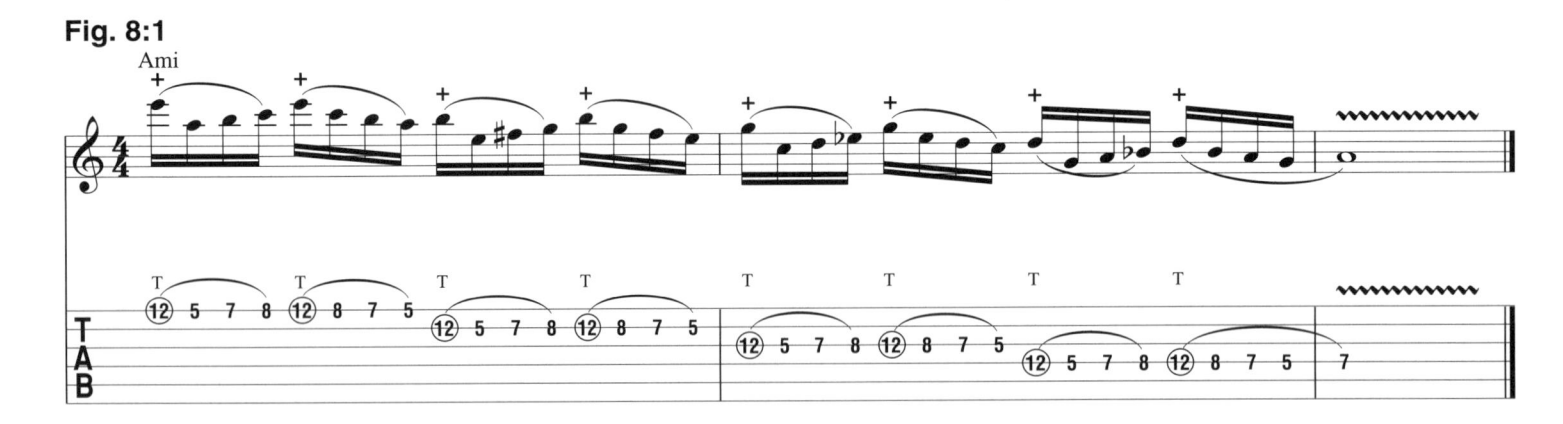

Track 49

Fig. 8:1

Fig. 8:2 is another trademark tapping pattern from Eddie's arsenal. This one is based on A major (A–B–C#–D–E–F#–G#) and A Dorian properties.

Chapter 8

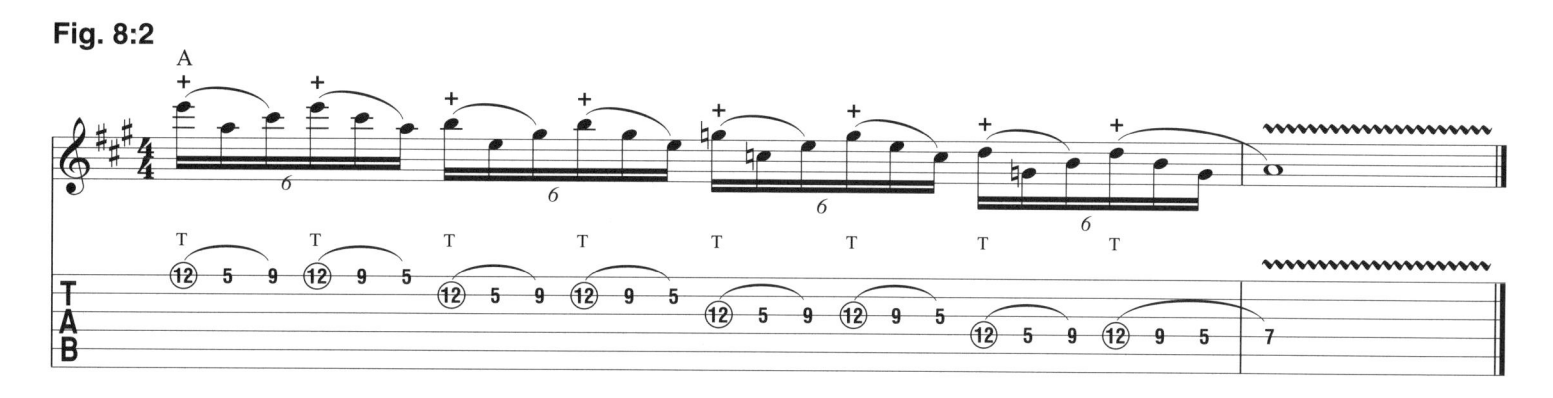

Track 50

Fig. 8:2

This Eddie-inspired shredfest (Fig. 8:3) contains elements of both the G major (G–A–B–C–D–E–F#) and G minor scale (G–A–B♭–C–D–E♭–F). The "10" notation means you'll need to pack ten notes into the space of eight 32nds!

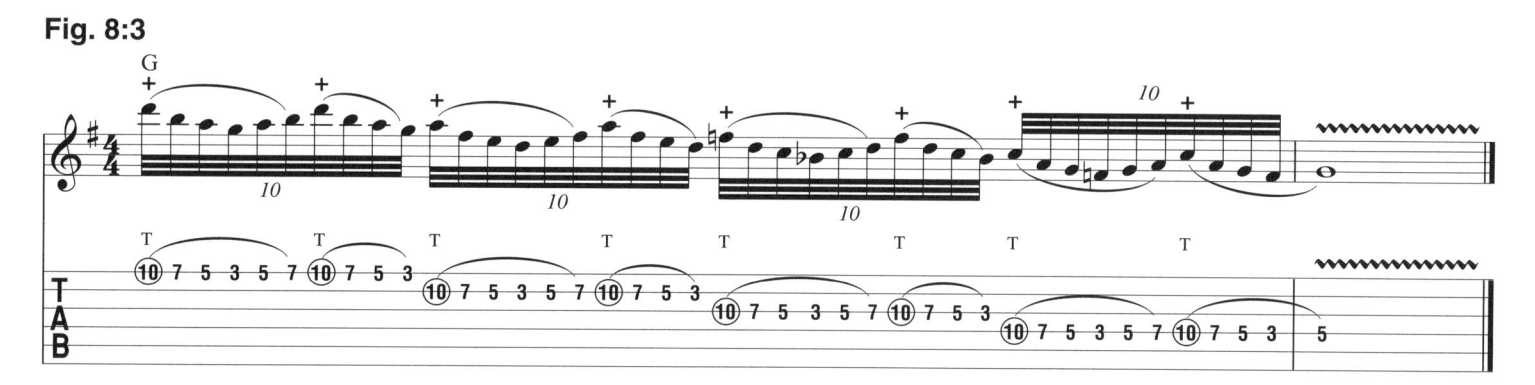

Track 51

Fig. 8:3

Check out these next several tapping ideas inspired by Greg Howe and Paul Gilbert (Figs. 8:4–8:6). All three are derived exclusively from the A minor scale. (In the first measure of Fig. 8:5, each three-note grouping begins with a hammer-on from nowhere.)

Track 52
(0:00)

Fig. 8:4

8

Track 52
(0:06)

Fig. 8:5

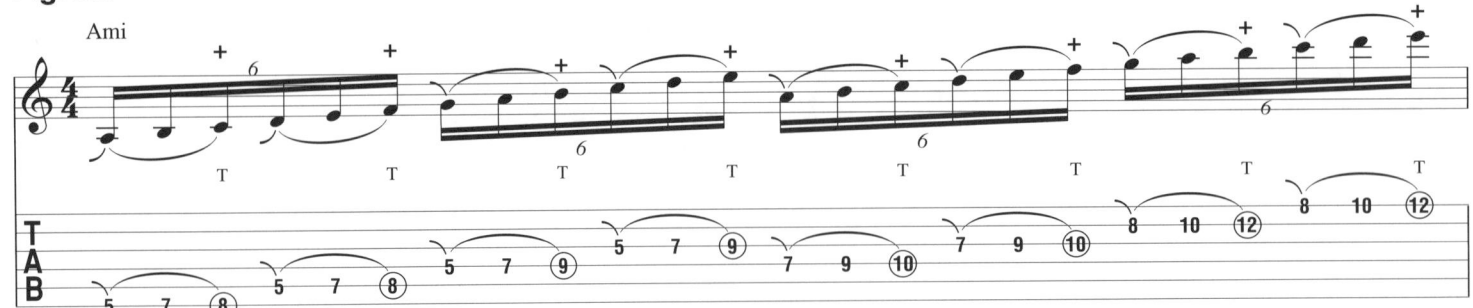

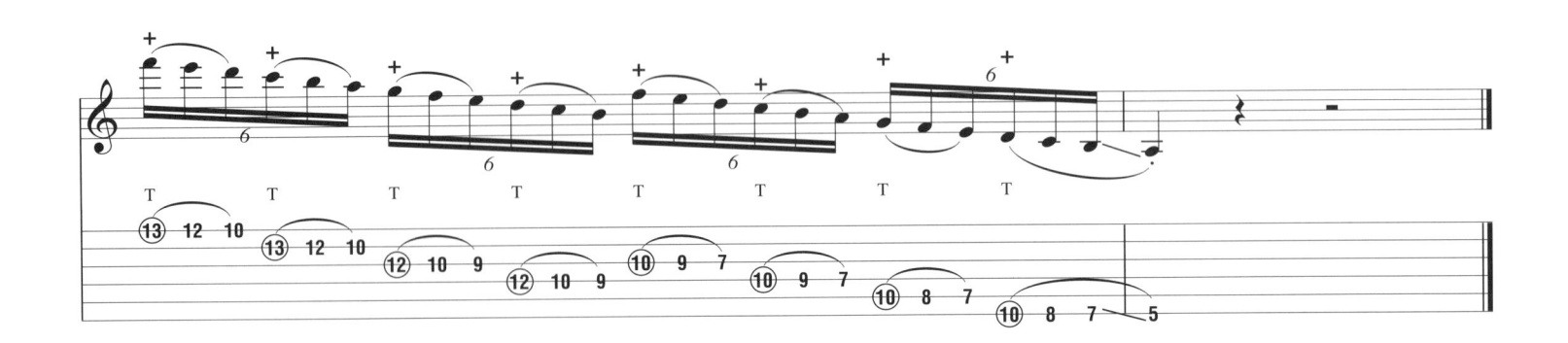

Track 52
(0:13)

Fig. 8:6

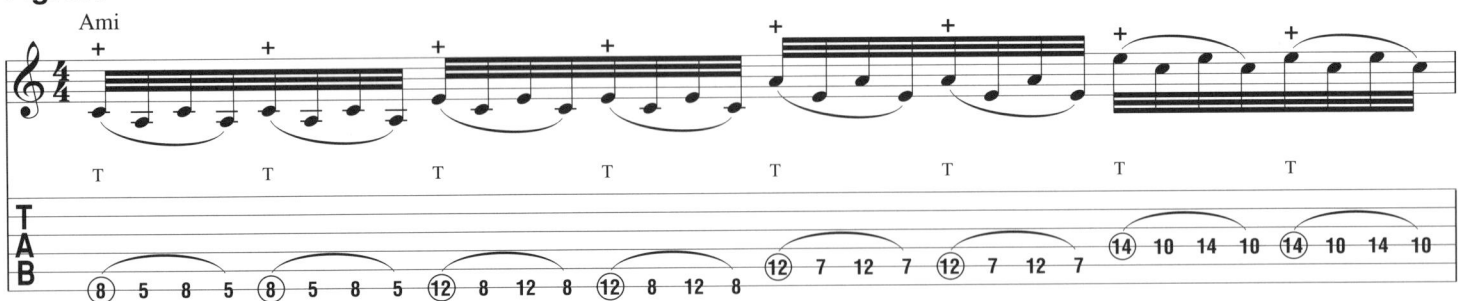

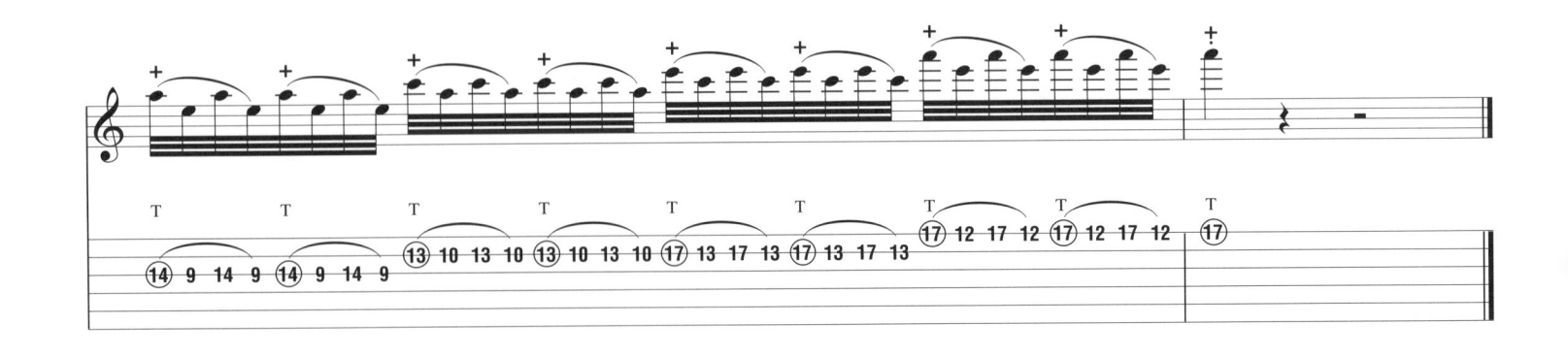

Chapter 8

Fig. 8:7 is a classic example of Eddie Van Halen's approach to arpeggios. Dmi (D–F–A) and B7 (B–D♯–F♯–A) arpeggios open the example in measure 1, followed by Emi (E–G–B) and F major (F–A–C) triads in measure 2. A G° triad (G–B♭–D♭[C♯]) provides tension over the A7 chord in measure 3, and the example goes out on a resolving D note.

Track 53 (0:00)

Fig. 8:7

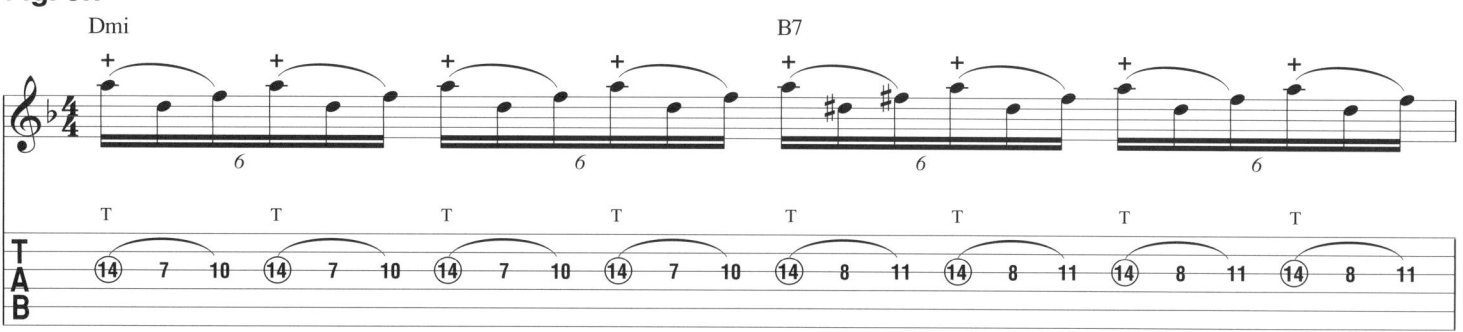

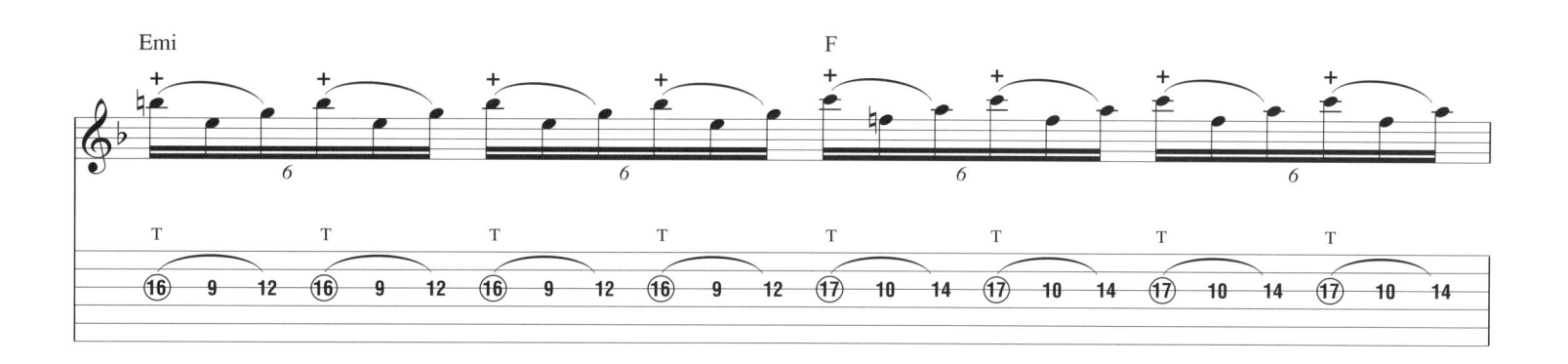

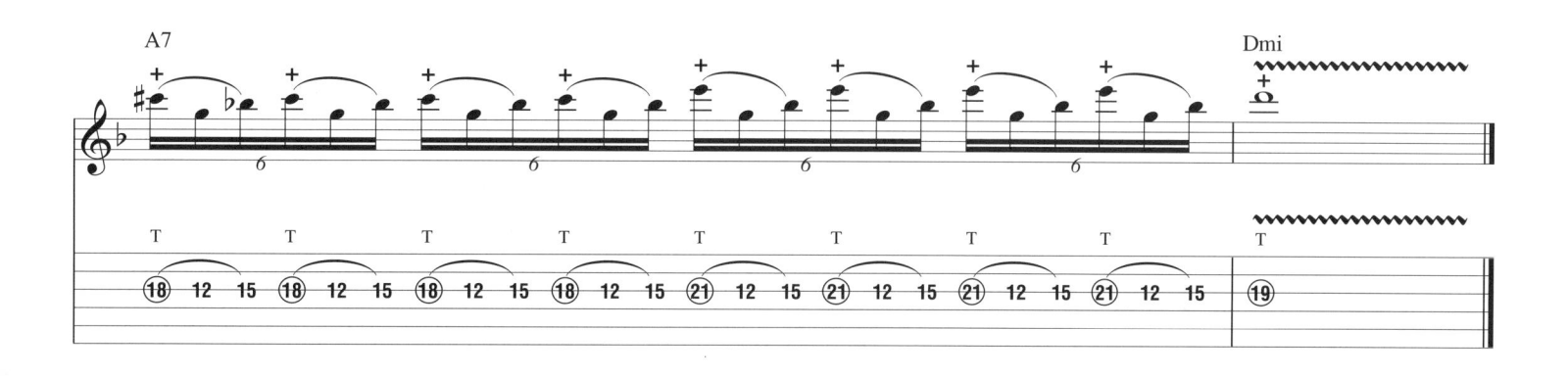

Fig. 8:8 is another Eddie-inspired example. Here, Emi (E–G–B), B7 (B–D#–F#–A), D major (D–F#–A), Dmi (D–F–A), E7 (E–G#–B–D), and A major (A–C#–E) triads and arpeggios directly outline each chord change.

Track 53
(0:10)

Fig. 8:8

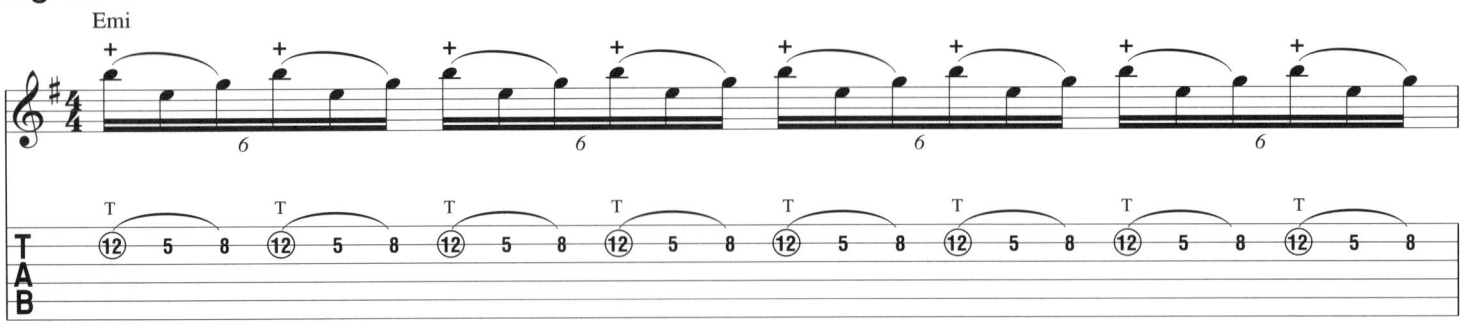

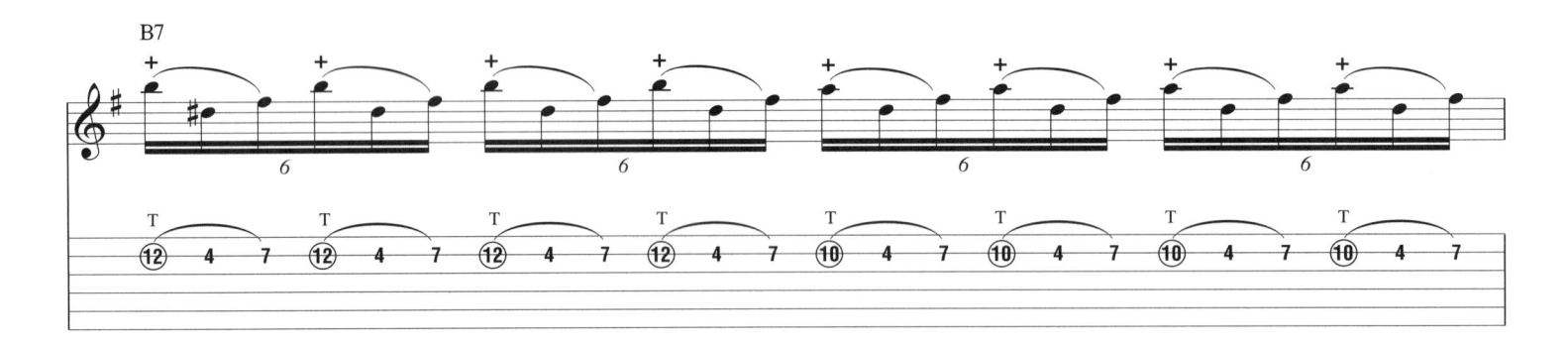

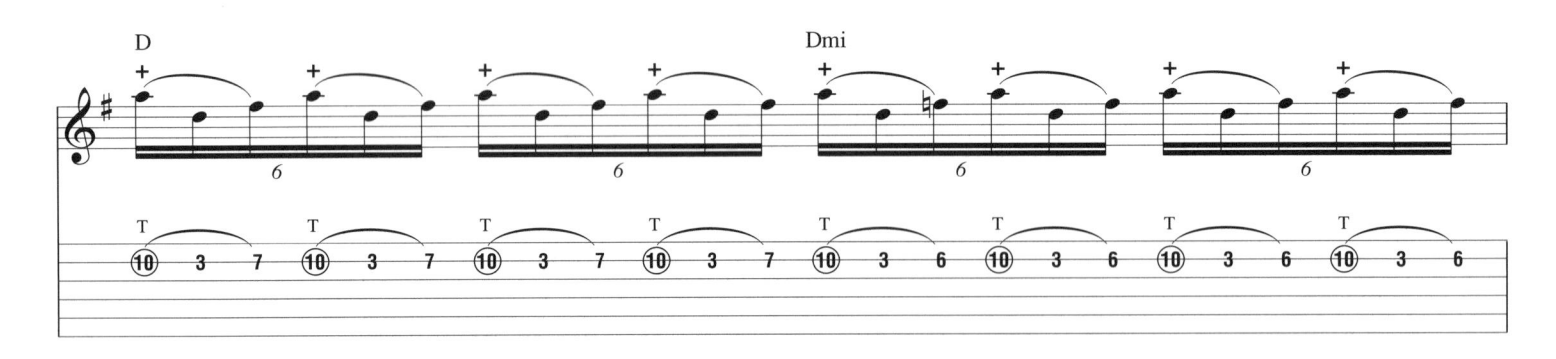

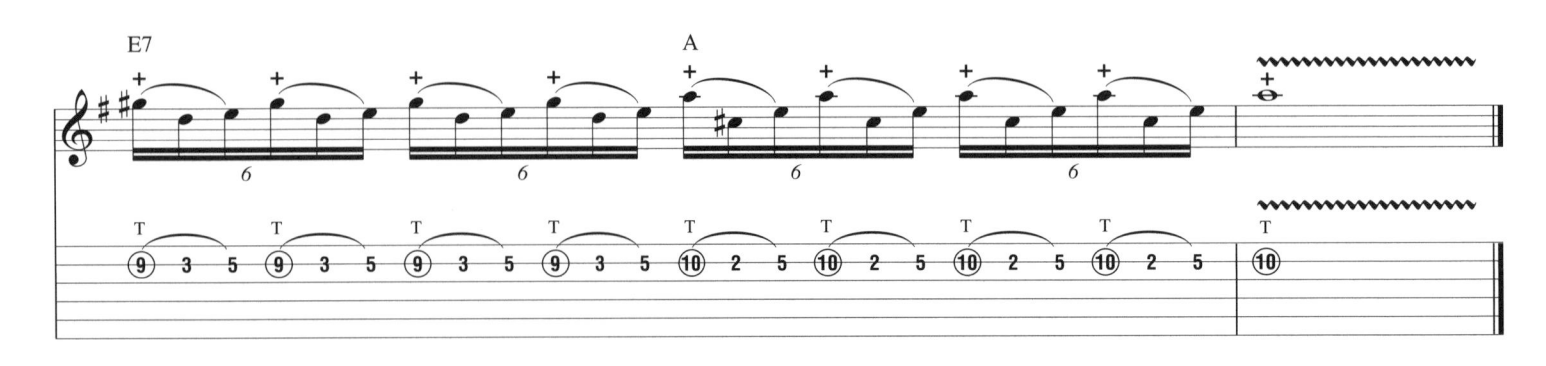

Chapter 8

The following two examples feature more advanced tapping ideas that use multiple arpeggio patterns. The first (Fig. 8:9) uses Ami triad inversions; the second (Fig. 8:10) employs an Fma7 arpeggio (F–A–C–E).

Track 54
(0:00)

Fig. 8:9

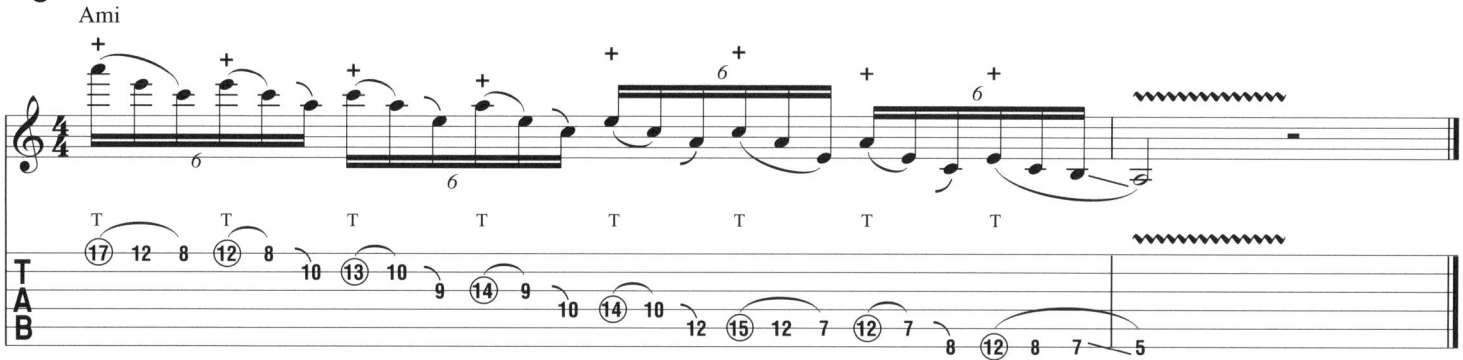

Track 54
(0:07)

Fig. 8:10

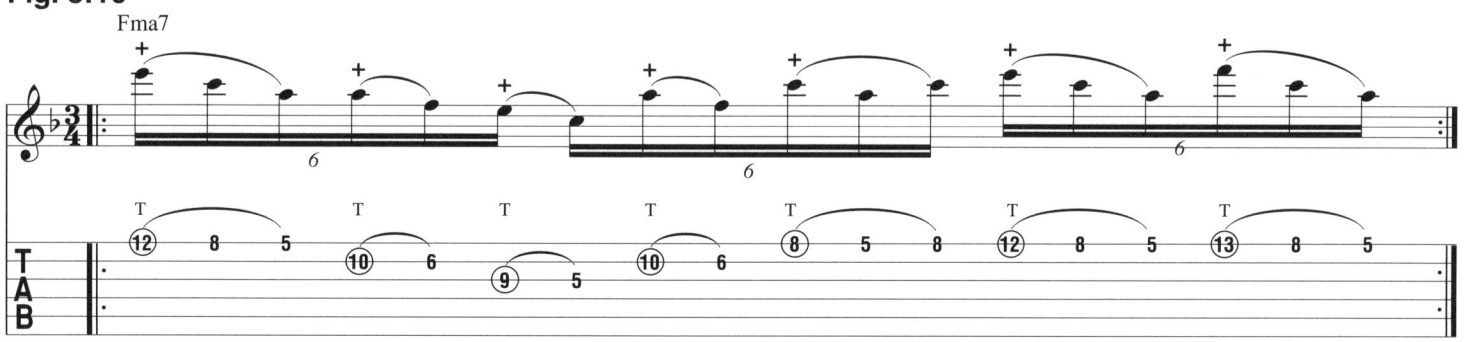

We'll close out with an A minor etude based on the tapping techniques set forth in this chapter. Constructed exclusively from arpeggios (Dmi9, Cma9, Fma7, E7, and Ami), the piece relies heavily on the advanced tapping patterns introduced in Figs. 8:9 and 8:10. Again, put the etude together very slowly, measure-by-measure, until you get the feel for the tapping patterns. Then, and only then, should you start to increase the metronome setting. Be patient with yourself, and try not to get frustrated.

Fig. 8:11

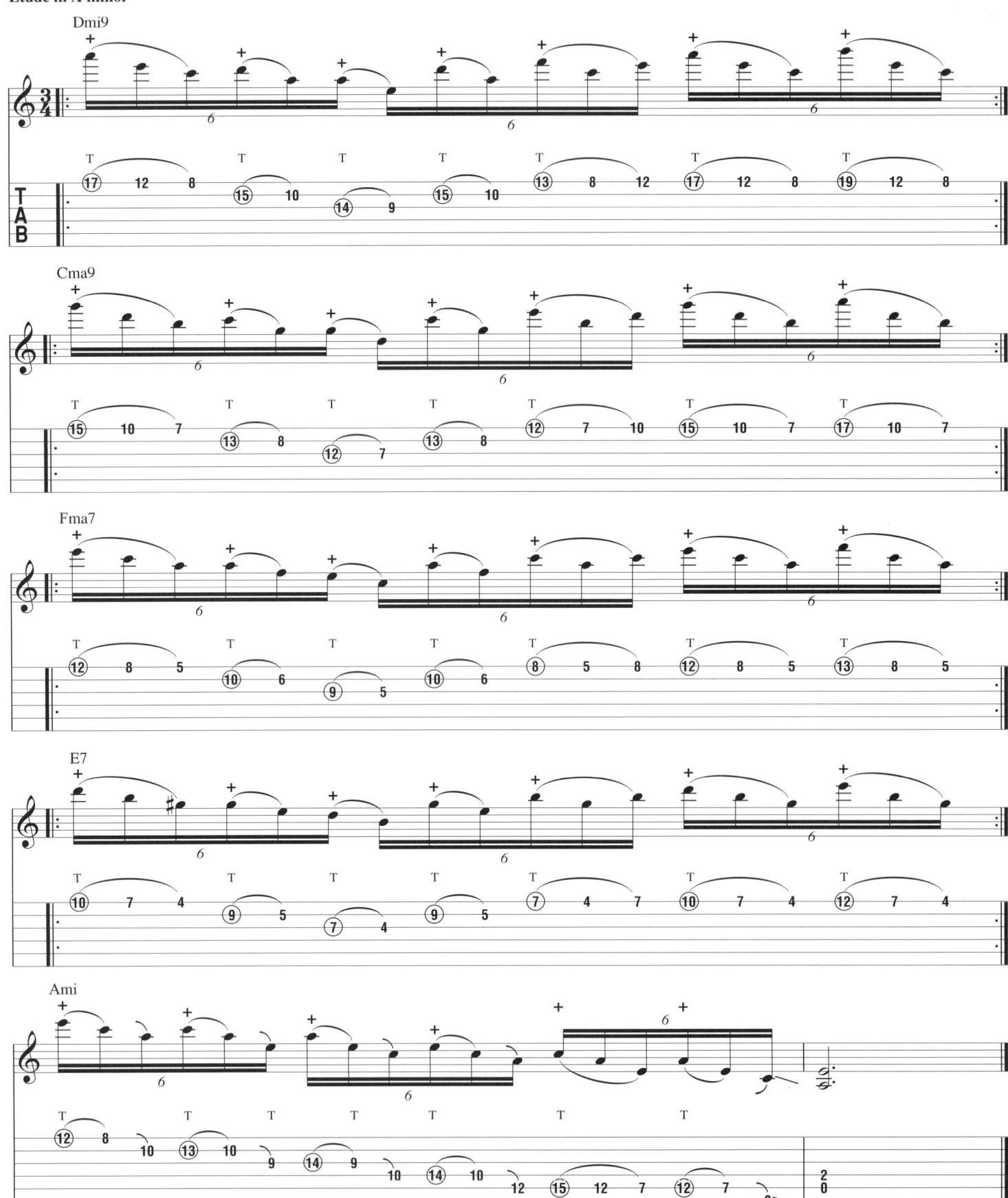

Etude in A minor

Extended Arpeggios

9

This chapter will focus on creating extended arpeggios with help of diatonic substitutions (triads and arpeggios from the same key center). The process should help to further your knowledge of how the fretboard works. We'll be applying the concepts from previous chapters to execute these arpeggios fluently. [Note: If you don't have a grasp on diatonic substitutions, I suggest you refer to a good music theory book, such as *Music Theory for Guitarists* from Hal Leonard Publishing.]

Combining Two Triads

Let's start with an example (Fig. 9:1) that combines a root-position Ami triad (A–C–E) with a second-inversion C major triad (G–C–E; 5th–root–3rd). (Ami (i) is the harmony of the root of the A minor scale; C (♭III) is the harmony of third scale step.) Combining these two triads results in an Ami7 arpeggio (A–C–E–G). [Note: The examples in this chapter all gravitate towards sweep-picking techniques. For this reason, I've included suggested picking directions; however, this doesn't mean you shouldn't experiment with other picking options.]

Track 56

Fig. 9:1

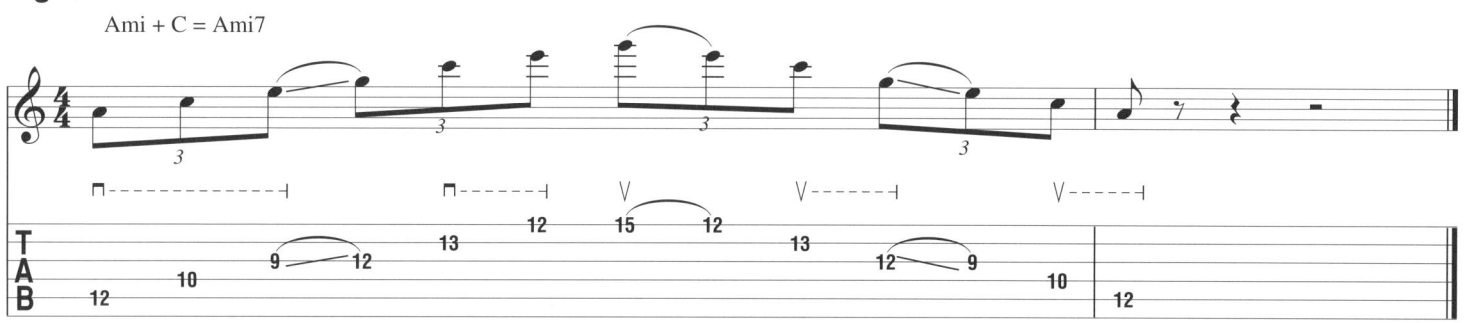

Fig. 9:2 shows how, by including the tonic note (A) in each octave, we arrive at a two-octave Ami7 arpeggio shape.

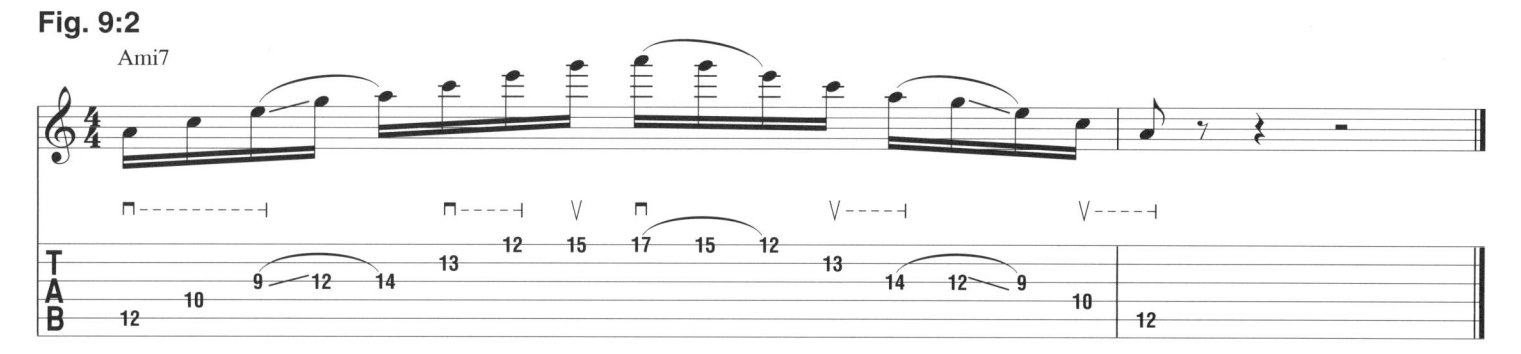

Track 57

Fig. 9:2

Fig. 9:3 mates a C major triad with a second-inversion Emi triad (B–E–G; 5th–root–♭3rd) for a Cma7 (C–E–G–B) outcome. (C and Emi are the I and iii (triad) chord harmony of the C major scale.)

Track 58

Fig. 9:3

C + Emi = Cma7

Plug in the missing tonic notes (C) and you have a straight-ahead trip up and down a two-octave Cma7 arpeggio (Fig. 9:4).

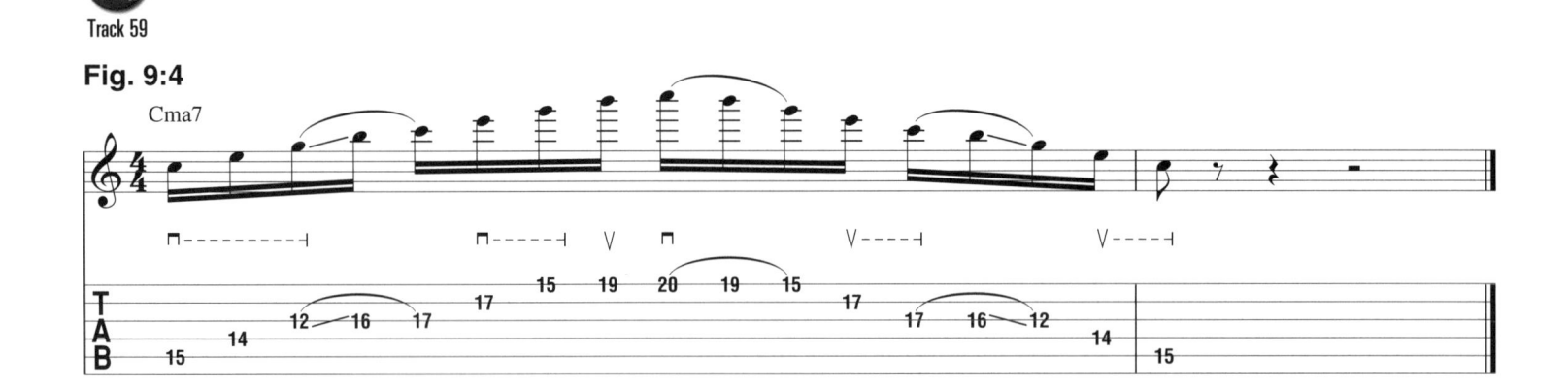

Track 59

Fig. 9:4

Cma7

Fig. 9:5 tacks a G major triad (G–B–D) onto an F major triad (F–A–C) for a G11 tonality (G–B–C–D–F–A). (G and F are the triad harmony of the root and ♭7th degrees of the G Mixolydian mode: G–A–B–C–D–E–F; fifth mode of C major.)

Track 60

Fig. 9:5

G + F = G11

Chapter 9

Fig. 9:6 puts an interesting twist on the previous example.

Track 61

Fig. 9:6

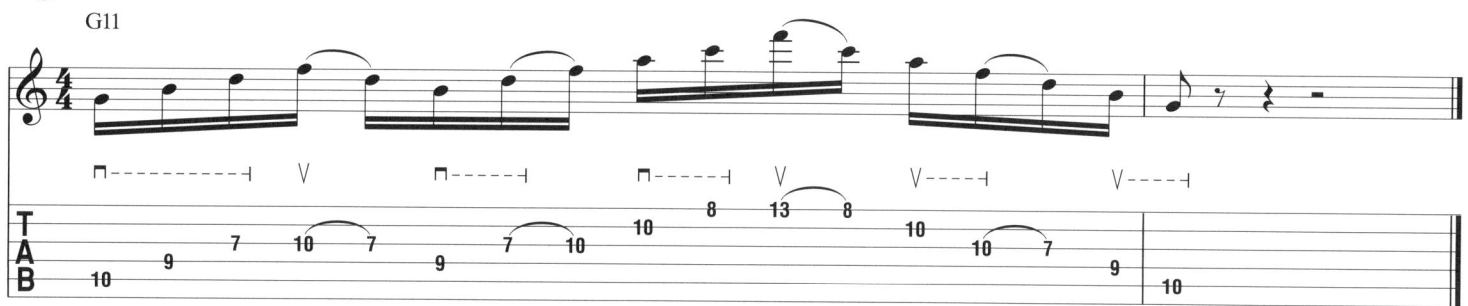

Combining Seventh Arpeggios

Combining seventh arpeggios produces an even richer sound. In Fig. 9:7, a Cmi7 arpeggio (C–E♭–G–B♭) segues to an E♭ma7 (E♭–G–B♭–D). The result is a Cmi9 (C–E♭–G–B♭–D) tonality. (Cmi7 is the seventh chord quality of the i chord in the C minor scale (C–D–E♭–F–G–A♭–B♭); E♭ma7 is the ♭III chord harmony.)

Track 62

Fig. 9:7

Cmi7 + E♭ma7 = Cmi9

Fig. 9:8 fuses a Cmi7 (C–E♭–G–B♭) with a second-inversion Gmi7 arpeggio (D–F–G–B♭; 5th–♭7th–root–♭3rd). The combination of these arpeggios implies a Cmi11 (C–E♭–G–B♭–D–F) tonality. (Cmi7 and Gmi7 are the harmony of the first and fifth degrees of the C minor scale.)

Track 63

Fig. 9:8

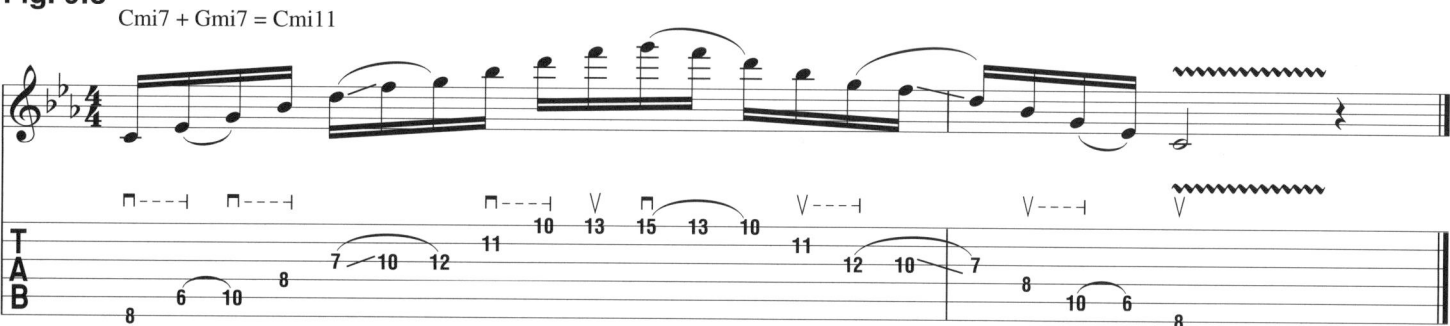

Cmi7 + Gmi7 = Cmi11

In Fig. 9:9, a common tone (F) links a Gmi7 (G–B♭–D–F) to an Fma7 (F–A–C–E) for a Gmi13 outcome (G–B♭–D–F–A–C–E). (Gmi7 and Fma7 are the harmonies of the root and ♭7th degrees of the G Dorian mode [G–A–B♭–C–D–E–F; second mode of F major].)

Track 64

Fig. 9:9
Gmi7 + Fma7 = Gmi13

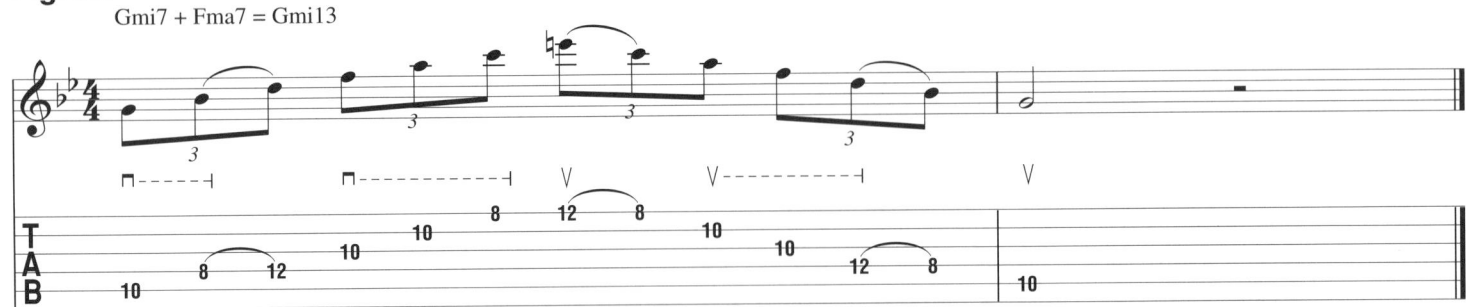

Extended Arpeggios with Tapping

We'll wrap things up with some "extension producing" tapping examples. Fig. 9:10 begins with a Gma7 (G–B–D–F♯) tapping lick (first three beats), then adds a ninth extension (A) with a tap to the 17th fret of the high-E string (on beat 4).

Track 65

Fig. 9:10
Gma9

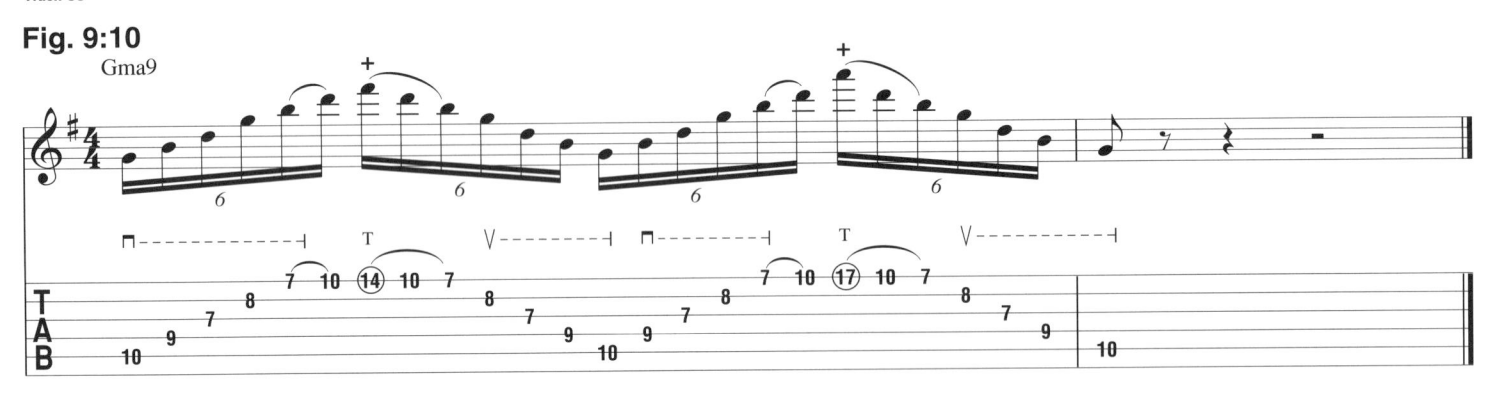

In Fig. 9:11, tapping to the "B" notes morphs a C6 arpeggio (C–E–G–A) into a Cma9 arpeggio (C–E–G–B–A).

Track 66

Fig. 9:11
Cma13

m = middle finger
a = ring finger

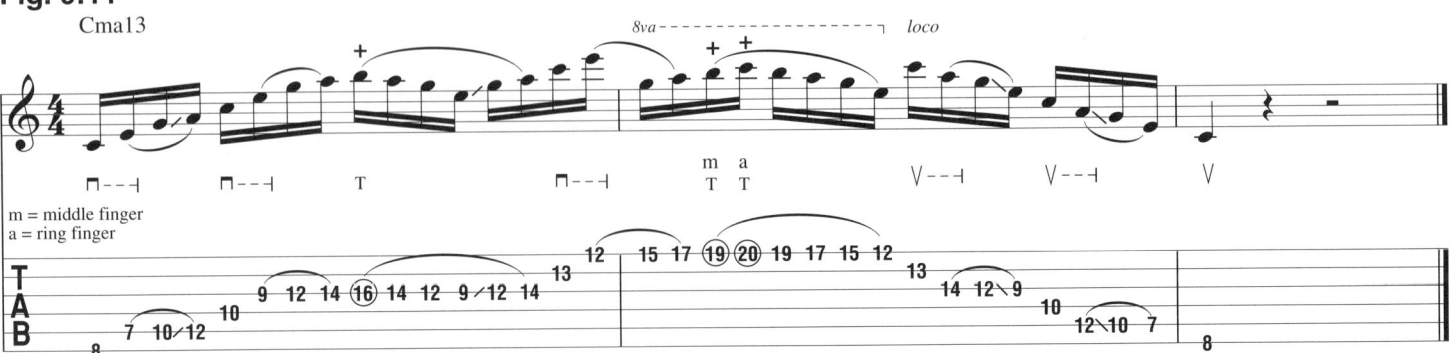

Chapter 9

A tap to the F# note emphasizes the "dominant 13th" quality of this A13(#11) (A–C#–E–G–B–D#–F#) example (Fig. 9:12).

Track 67

Fig. 9:12

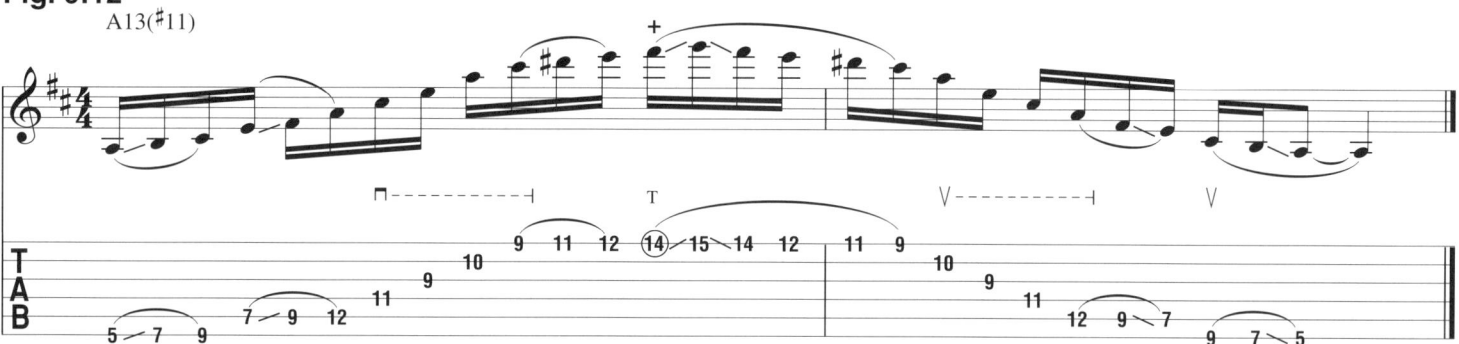

A13(#11)

Here's an "inside/outside" tap/slide lick (Fig. 9:13) based on an Am9(♭13/#11) arpeggio (A–C–E–G–B–D#–F). After tapping the high-E string at the 13th fret, slide your tapping finger up to the 16th fret and back down to the 13th, then perform the pull-offs with your fret-hand fingers.

Track 68

Fig. 9:13

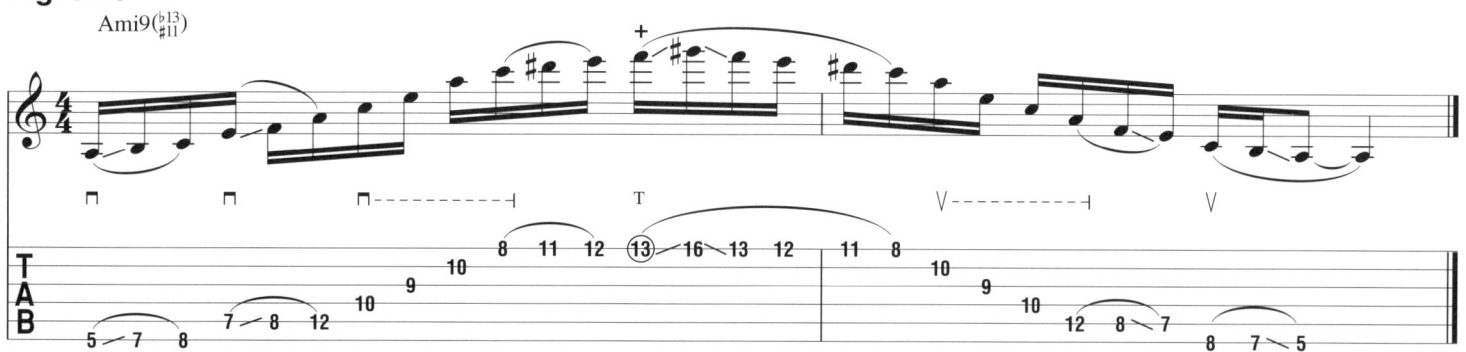

Ami9(♭13/#11)

I encourage you to take these concepts and expand upon them. Try combining different arpeggios, keeping track of the sounds you like. Keep in mind: experimentation is key to your growth as a musician.

10 Odd Groupings/ Hybrid Picking

In this chapter, we'll be covering two of my favorite topics: odd groupings and hybrid picking.

Odd Groupings

The unpredictable sound of odd groupings can add a new dimension to your improvisations. These groupings seem to "float" through time, and are sometimes extremely difficult to play. Here's a practice tip that should help you to get a handle on odd groupings. First, let's play a repeating five-note lick using sixteenth notes (Fig. 10:1A).

Track 69

Fig. 10:1A
A Blues Scale

Now let's take that same lick and cram all five notes into each beat (Fig. 10:1B).

Track 70

Fig. 10:1B
A Blues Scale

I suggest utilizing this approach whenever you find yourself struggling to play irregular groupings. Let's look at one more example before moving on. Here's a seven-note lick played in groups of four sixteenth notes (Fig. 10:2A).

Track 71

Fig. 10:2A

A Blues Scale

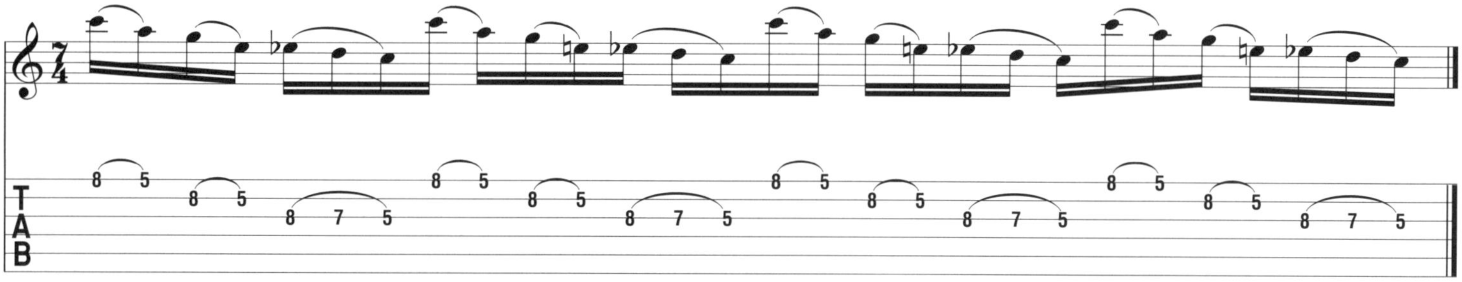

Now here's the same lick, but played in seven-against-six (seven notes played in the space of six sixteenth notes).

Track 72

Fig. 10:2B

A Blues Scale

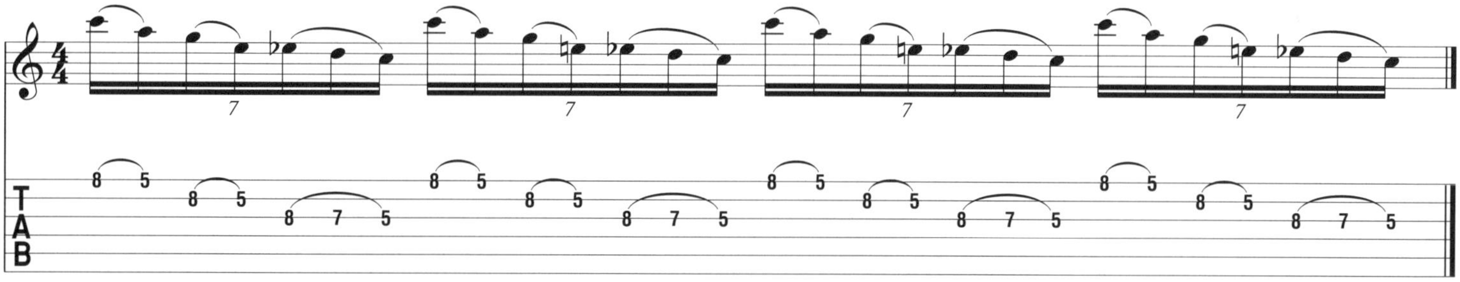

Hybrid Picking

Hybrid picking is what I consider a shredder's secret weapon. Instead of just using your pick, use your fingers too! This technique not only makes string skipping far easier, but also adds a nice "snap" to your licks. Check out the string-skipping lick in Fig. 10:3A.

Track 73

Fig. 10:3A

A Major Scale

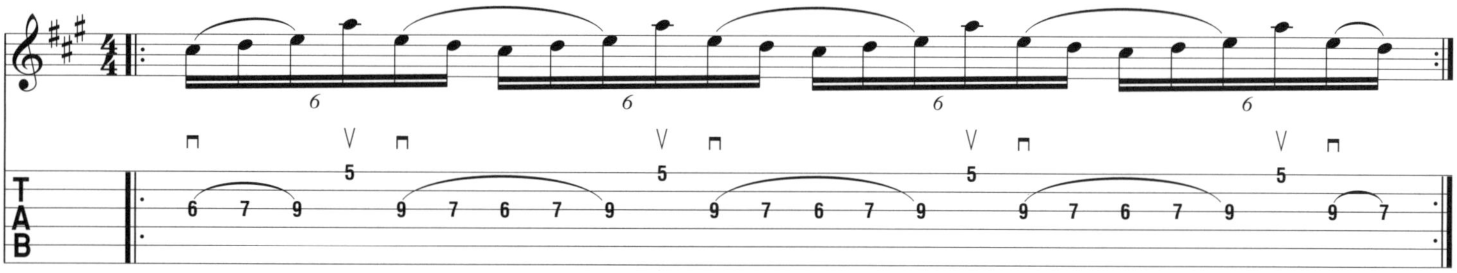

Now, let's play the lick using hybrid picking. Pick down on the G string with the pick, and pluck up on the high-E string using the middle finger of your fret hand (Fig. 10:3B).

Track 74

Fig. 10:3B
A Major Scale

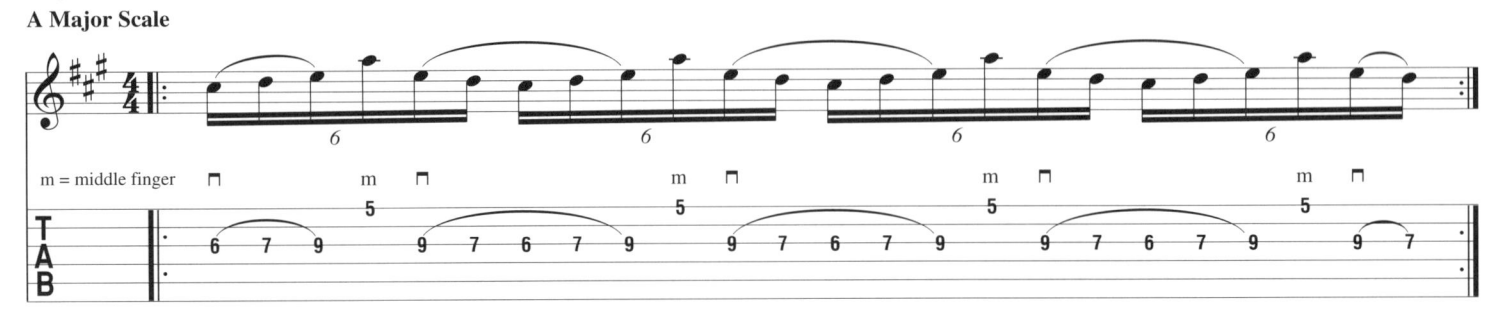

m = middle finger

The extra dynamic that this technique offers is very attention-getting as well as practical. Let's apply hybrid picking to the odd grouping exercises we played earlier in this chapter. For Fig. 10:4, pluck up on the B string with your middle finger and pick down on the G string with the pick. For Fig. 10:5, pluck up on the high-E string with your ring finger, pluck up on the B string with your middle finger, and pick down on the D string with the pick.

Track 75 (0:00)

Fig. 10:4
A Blues Scale

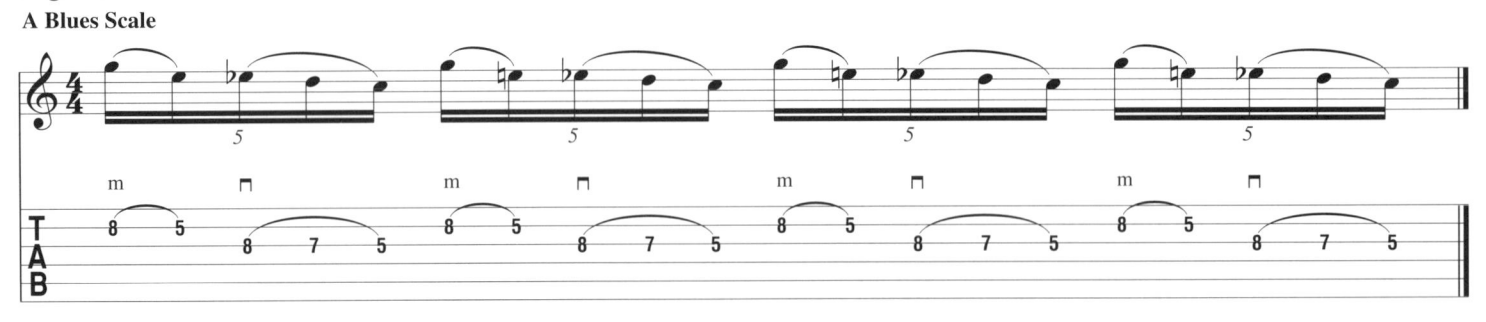

Track 75 (0:07)

Fig. 10:5
A Blues Scale

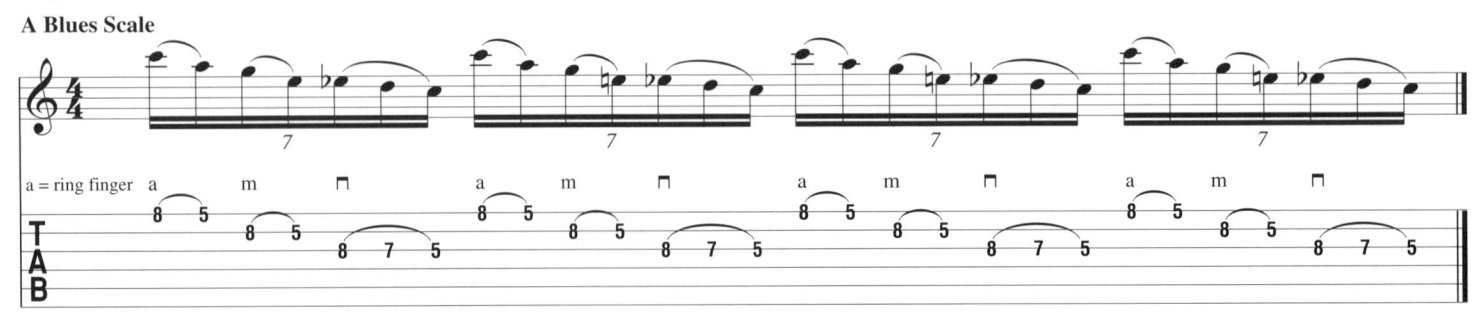

a = ring finger

62

Chapter 10

Mixed Examples

All of the following examples employ one or both of the topics covered in this chapter. First up is an A blues scale example using hybrid picking (Fig. 10:6).

Track 76

Fig. 10:6
A Blues Scale

Here's an A blues lick that uses both hybrid picking and odd groupings (Fig. 10:7).

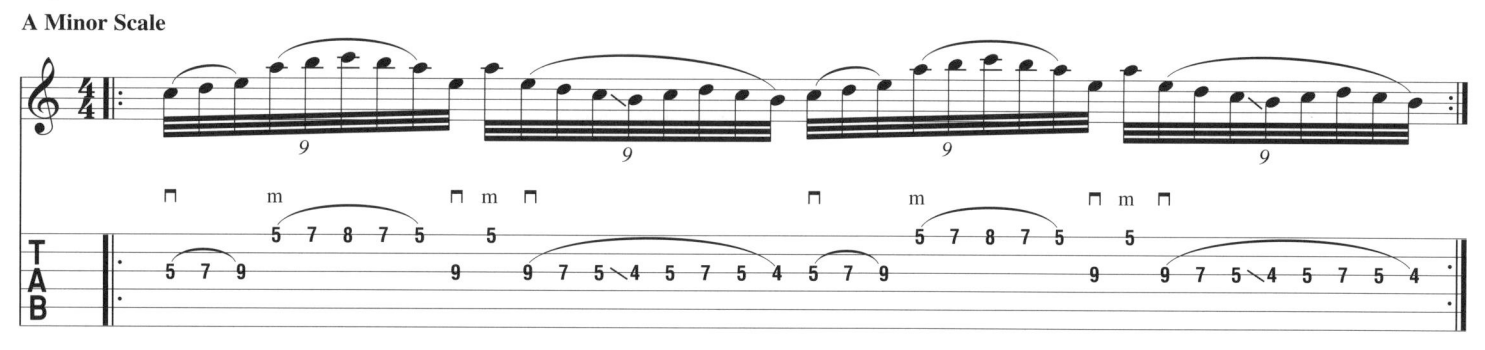

Track 77

Fig. 10:7
A Blues Scale

Fig. 10:8's hybrid-picking, string skipper lays out nine notes in the space of eight thirty-second notes. One way to work this up to speed is to first feel each one-beat grouping as three sets of triplets.

Track 78

Fig. 10:8
A Minor Scale

10

The A Dorian example in Fig. 10:9 crams eleven notes into the space of eight thirty-second notes! Needless to say, take this one nice and slow. Try putting it together in steady sixteenth notes at first.

Track 79

Fig. 10:9
A Dorian

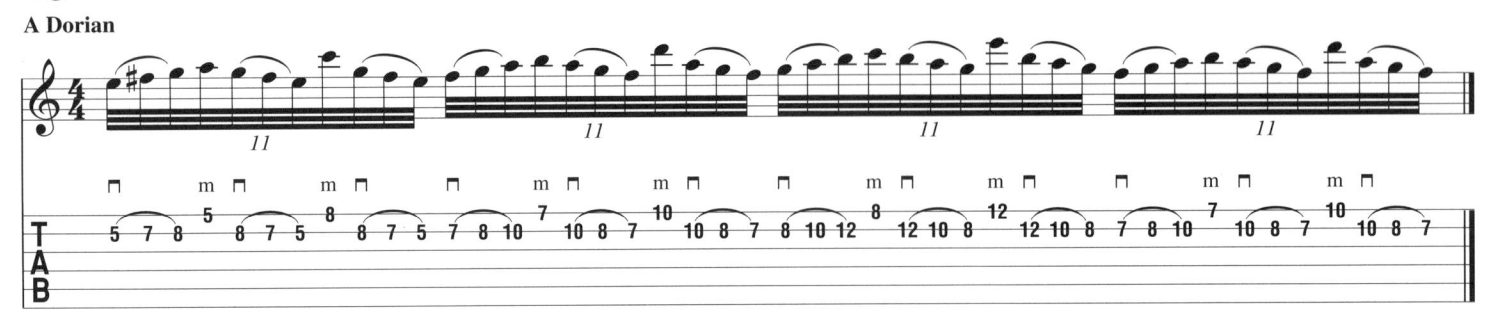

Fig. 10:10 is a hybrid-picked, string-skipping example that employs a C major triad and a B° triad.

Track 80

Fig. 10:10
C Major Triad   B° Triad

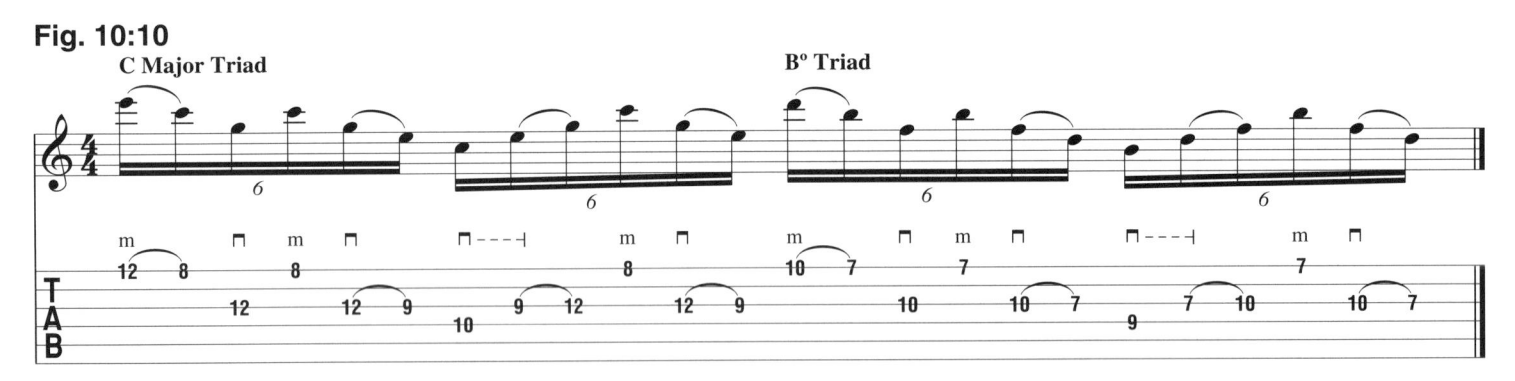

The C major scale receives the odd-grouping treatment in Fig. 10:11. Try putting it together using sixteenth notes at first—don't forget to use hybrid picking.

Track 81

Fig. 10:11
C Major Scale

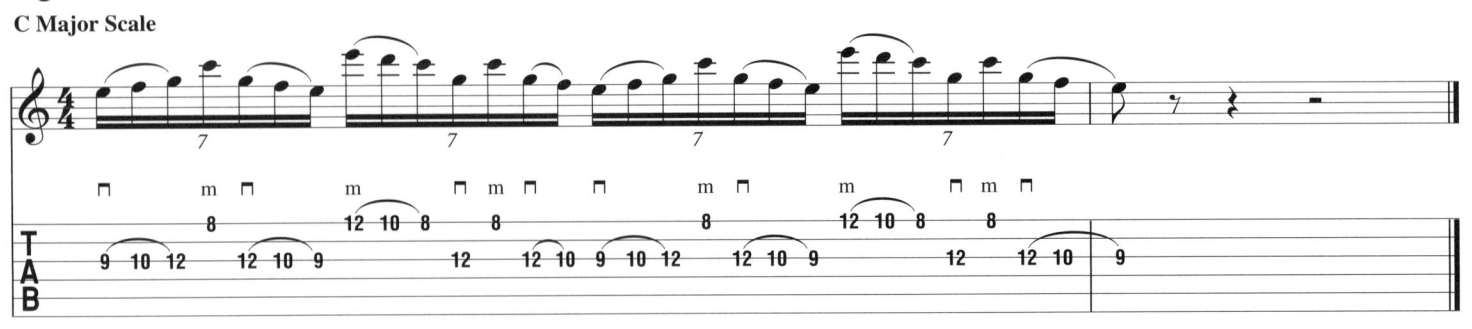

Chapter 10

Fig. 10:12 is a blazing A Dorian lick played with hybrid picking on the top two strings. Although odd groupings aren't in play here, the lick still has an uneven rhythmic structure.

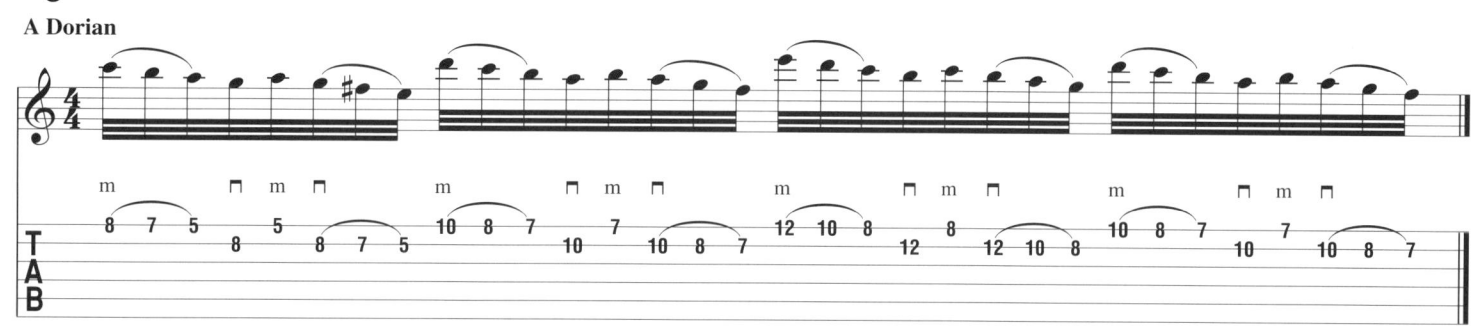

Track 82

Fig. 10:12
A Dorian

This final lick (Fig. 10:13) truly has a "free-floating" feel. With ten notes jammed into the space of eight thirty-seconds, it cascades down the C major scale in an adjacent-string pattern that repeats in each one-beat grouping.

Track 83

Fig. 10:13
C Major Scale

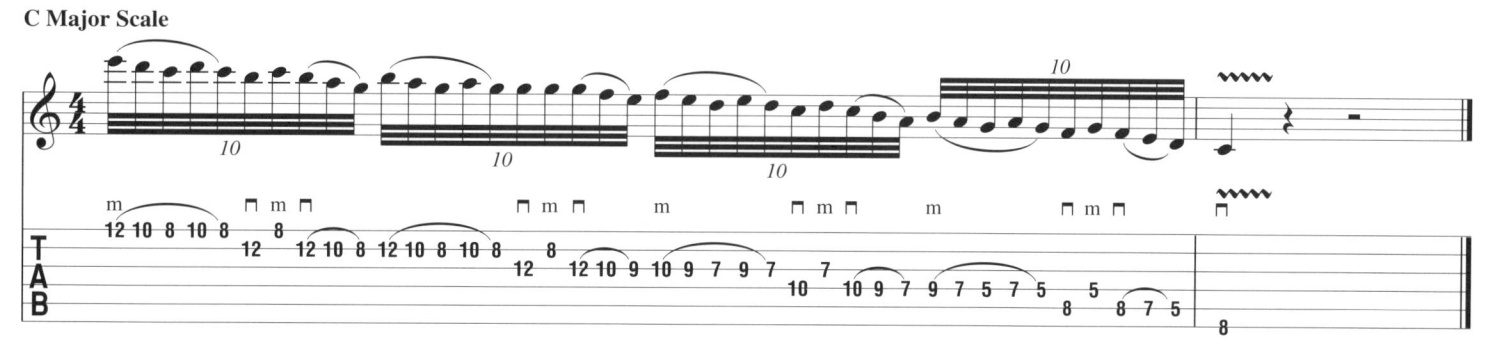

One final note: take these concepts and apply them to any of the previous chapters, and I'm sure you'll create something all your own. It's up to you to keep an open mind and experiment to find your own unique voice as a player.

11 Wide-Stretch Licks

Warning! Before attempting any of the examples in this chapter, you must stretch and warm up your hands. Never attempt wide stretches cold—serious injury can occur!

This final chapter covers wide fretting-hand stretches in scale and arpeggio form. These concepts will allow you to execute arpeggio sequences and wide intervallic phrases at speeds that would be impossible with traditional fingerings. We'll start with a lick that mixes the E minor (E–G–A–B–D) and E major pentatonic (E–F#–G#–B–C#) scales (Fig. 11:1). Because of the far-reaching requirements, I've included fret-hand fingering suggestions for all of the examples in this unit. Make sure you're warm and loose before you attempt it.

Track 84

Fig. 11:1

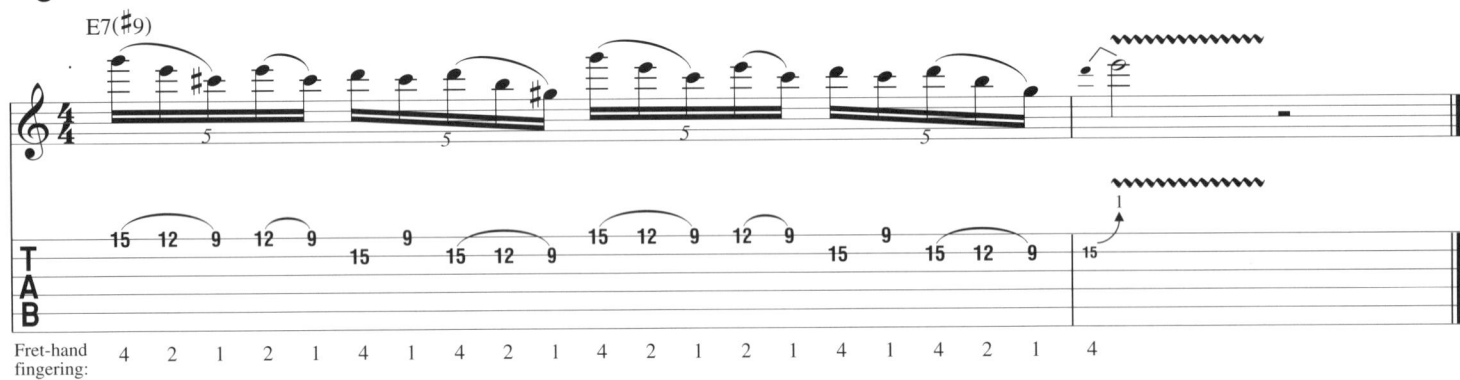

Fig. 11:2's stretcher contains elements of E Mixolydian (E–F#–G#–A–B–C#–D) and E blues (E–G–A–B♭–B–D).

Track 85

Fig. 11:2

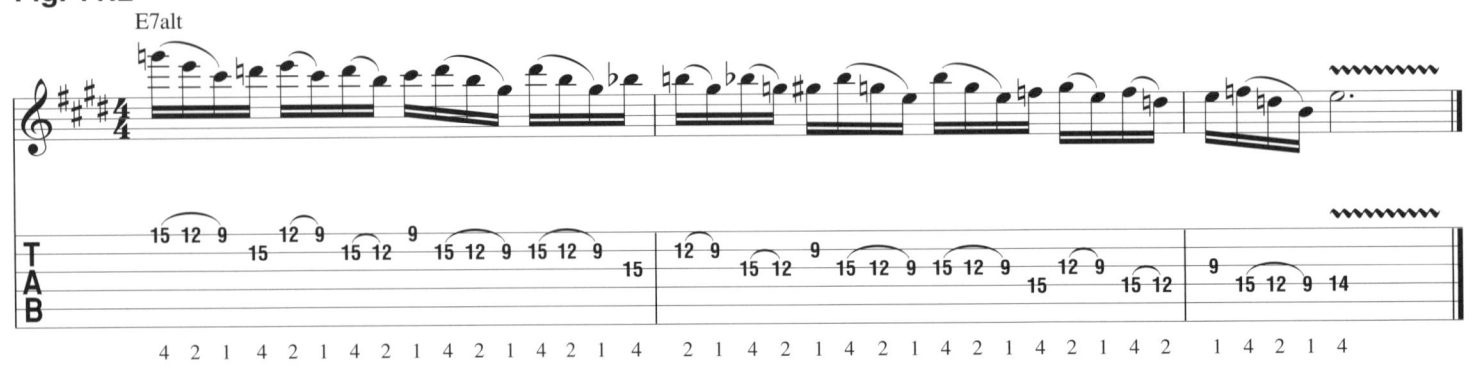

Chapter 11

Here's an E minor scale (E–F#–G–A–B–C–D) example that has a 4-fret spread at the top of the fretboard (Fig. 11:3).

Track 86

Fig. 11:3

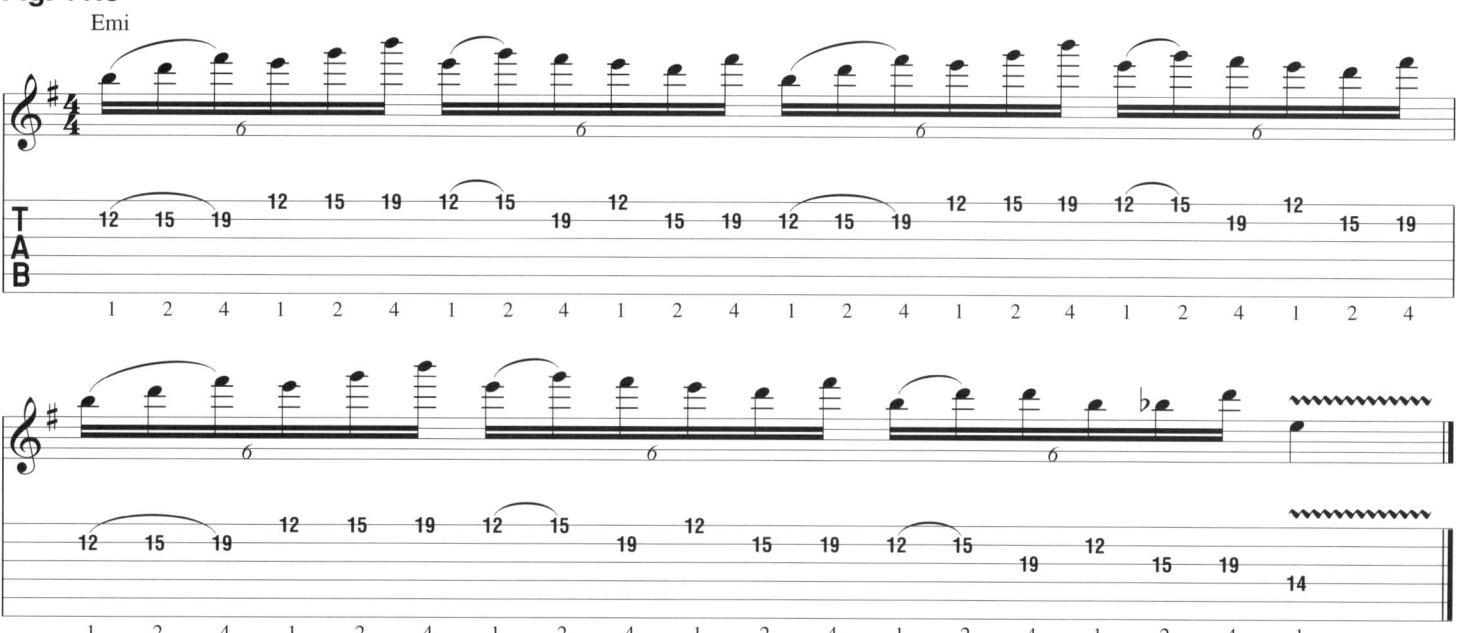

Here's a super-legato example that follows a set pattern (12th, 16th, and 19th frets) along each string (Fig. 11:4). The result is an interesting mix of E major (E–F#–G#–A–B–C#–D#), E Mixolydian, and E Dorian (E–F#–G–A–B–C#–D) scales. Use either your second or third finger to fret the 16th-fret notes.

Track 87

Fig. 11:4

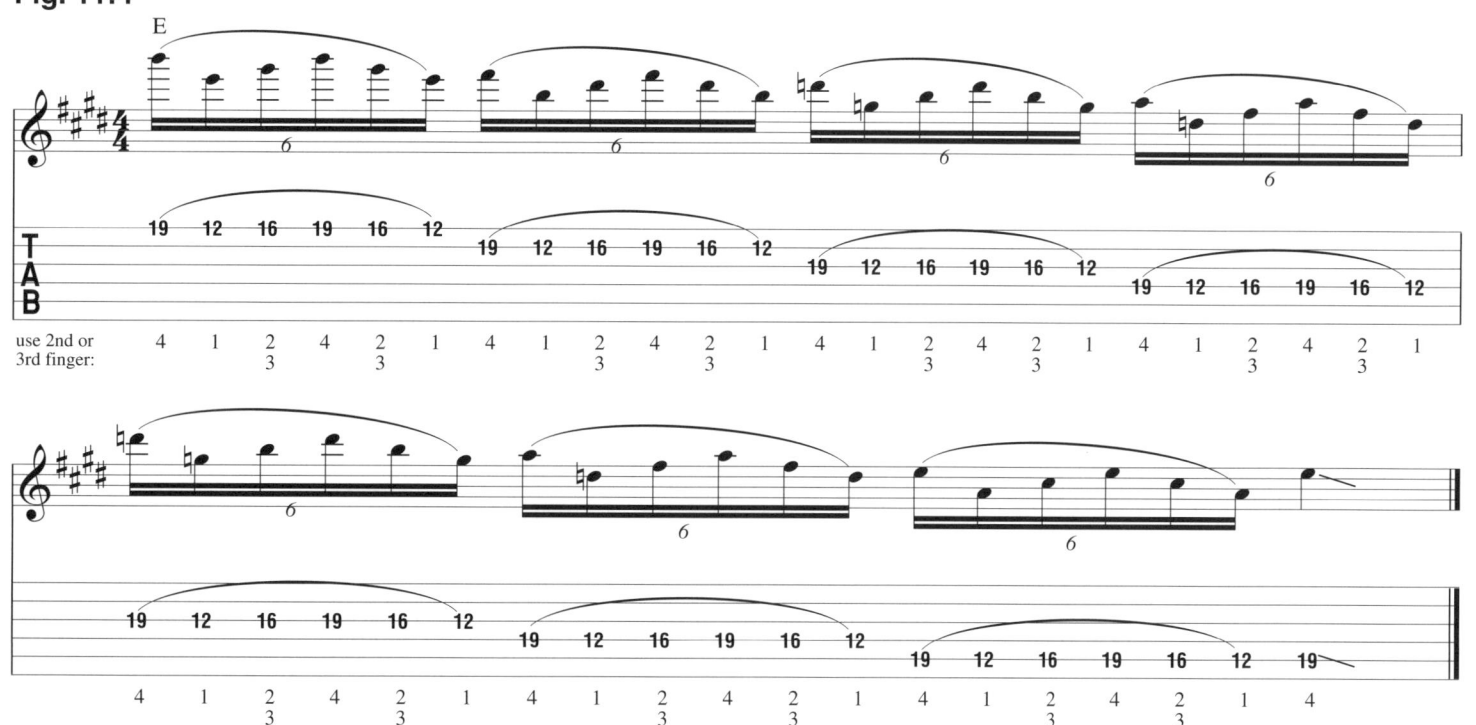

67

Fig. 11:5 is a challenging, E major-scale lick that contains some extreme five-fret spreads. Again, use the fingering that feels most comfortable to you.

Track 88

Fig. 11:5

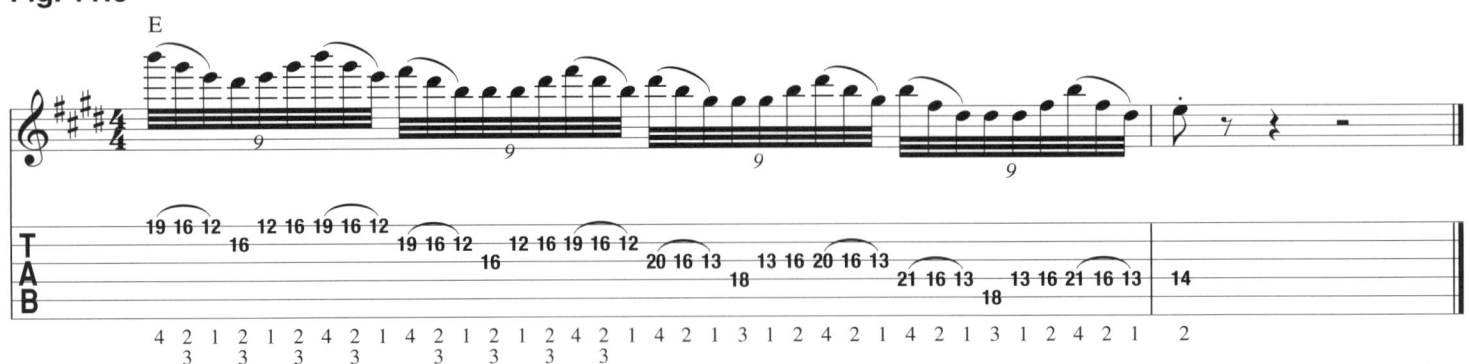

Here's a classical-sounding, pedal-point figure (Fig. 11:6) based on an E minor triad (E–G–B) and a B7 arpeggio (B–D#–F#–A).

Track 89

Fig. 11:6

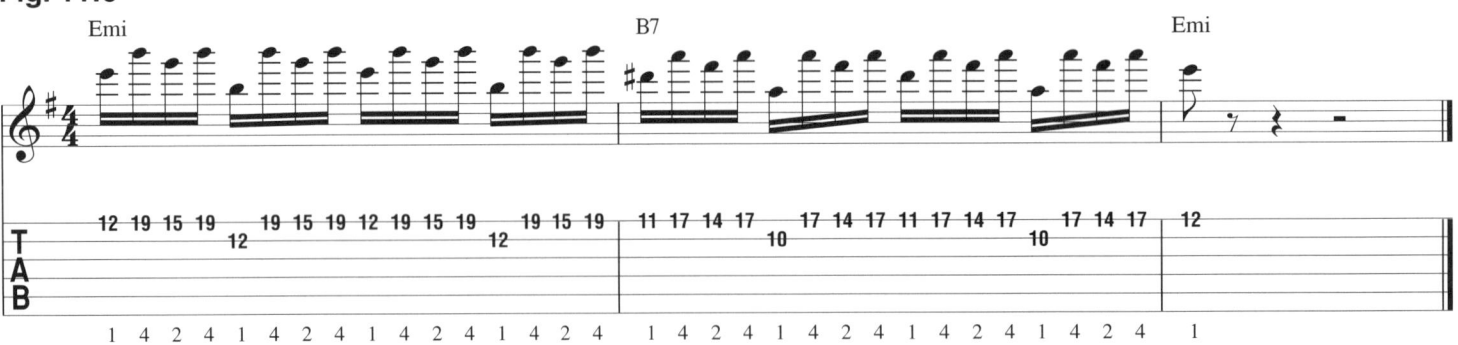

Fig. 11:7 is a string-skipping, wide-stretching example that superimposes a series of triads harmonized from the E minor scale: Emi (E–G–B), D (D–F#–A), Ami (A–C–E), G (G–B–D), and Bmi (B–D–F#).

Track 90

Fig. 11:7

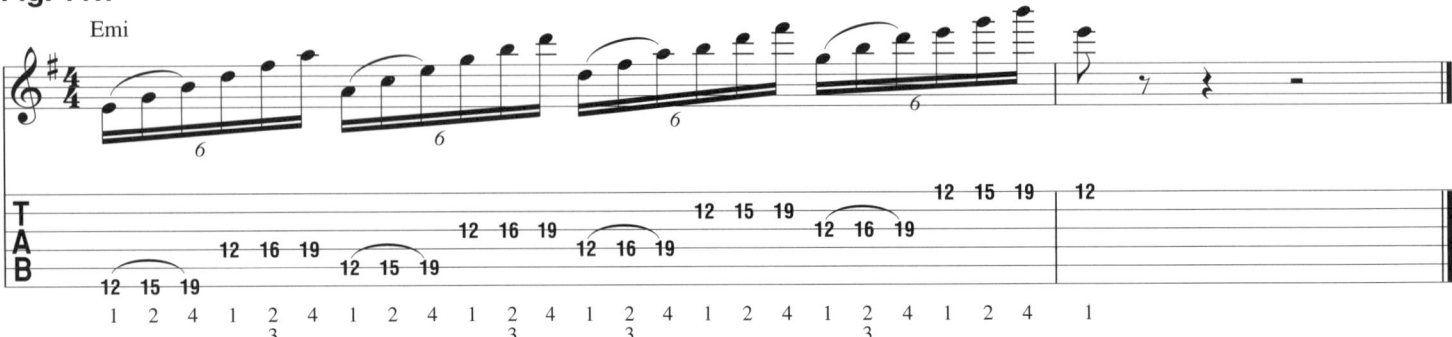

Chapter 11

Fig. 11:8 is another legato-fueled example, this time based on an Emi7 arpeggio (E–G–B–D). Don't miss that "tap" at the 22nd fret of the high-E string.

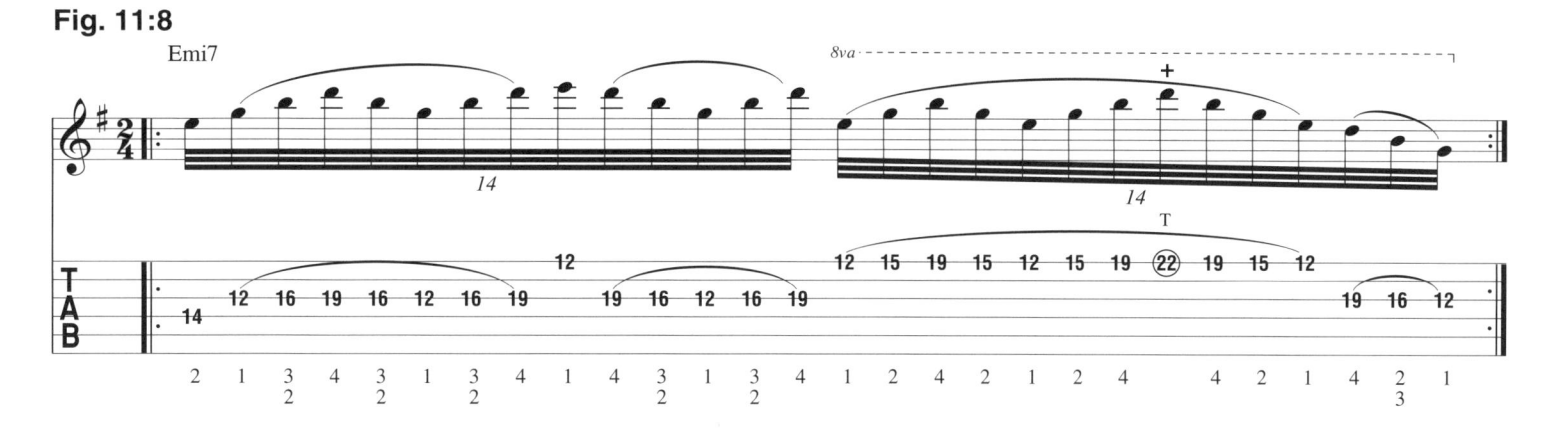

Track 91

Fig. 11:8

Fig. 11:9 is based on four-note-per-string fingerings. The stretches aren't as wide, but it still requires a considerable amount of dexterity.

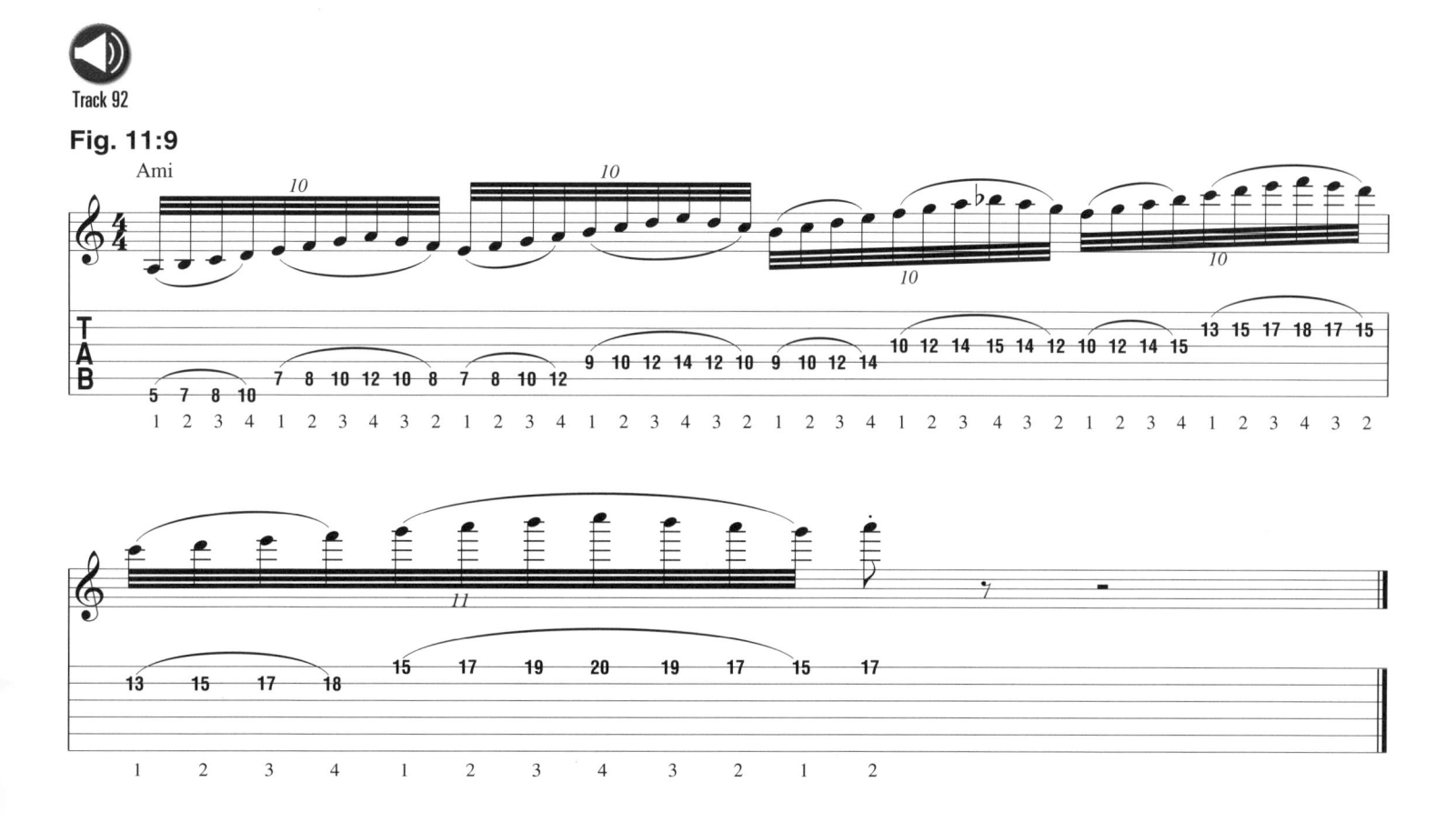

Track 92

Fig. 11:9

Here's another four-note-per-string lick (Fig. 11:10). Constructed from the E minor scale, it contains a series of string jumps.

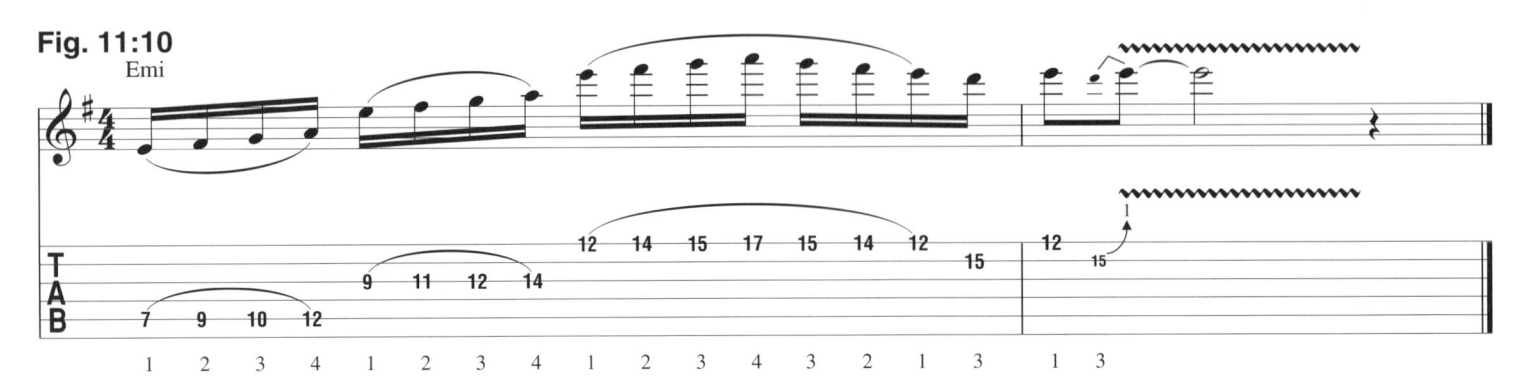

Track 93

Fig. 11:10

This last lick is pure, wide-stretch, string-skipping doom (Fig. 11:11). Have fun and good luck!

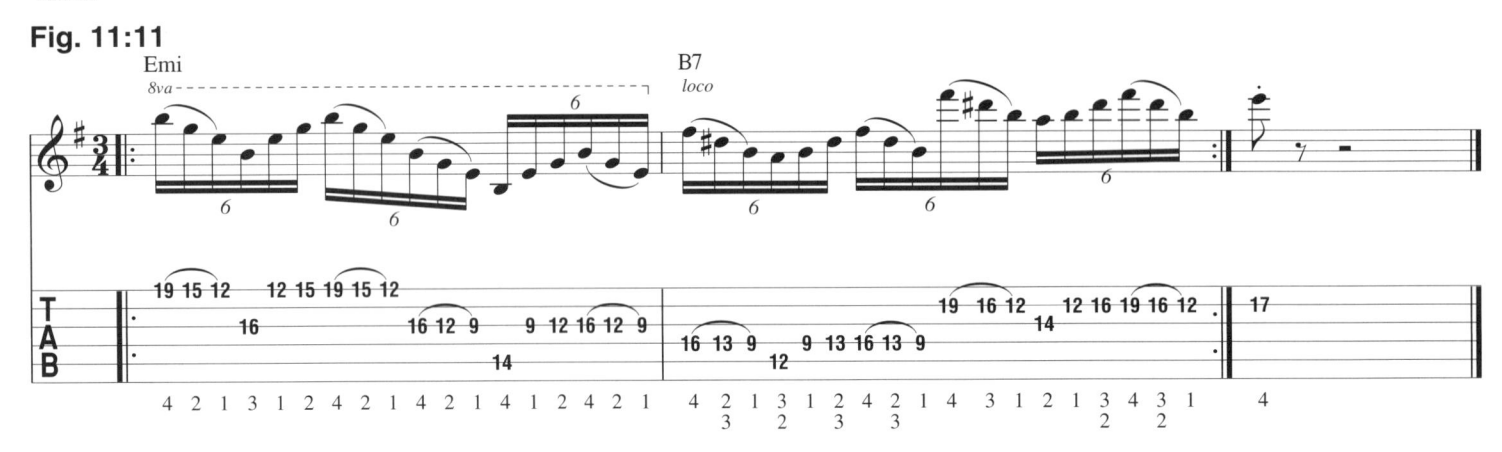

Track 94

Fig. 11:11

Track 95

The last audio track is my song titled "Epitaph of the Unborn." It combines elements of every chapter presented in this book. Enjoy!

MUSICIANS INSTITUTE PRESS is the official series of Southern California's renowned music school, Musicians Institute. MI instructors, some of the finest musicians in the world, share their vast knowledge and experience with you – no matter what your current level. For guitar, bass, drums, vocals, and keyboards, MI Press offers the finest music curriculum for higher learning through a variety of series:

ESSENTIAL CONCEPTS	MASTER CLASS	PRIVATE LESSONS
Designed from MI core curriculum programs.	Designed from MI elective courses.	Tackle a variety of topics "one-on-one" with MI faculty instructors.

BASS

Arpeggios for Bass
by Dave Keif • Private Lessons
00695133............................. $14.95

The Art of Walking Bass
by Bob Magnusson • Master Class
00695168 Book/CD Pack $18.95

Bass Fretboard Basics
by Paul Farnen • Essential Concepts
00695201............................. $16.95

Bass Playing Techniques
by Alexis Sklarevski • Essential Concepts
00695207............................. $16.95

Chords for Bass
by Dominik Hauser • Master Class
00695934 Book/CD Pack $16.95

Groove Mastery
by Oneida James • Private Lessons
00695771 Book/CD Pack $17.95

Grooves for Electric Bass
by David Keif • Private Lessons
00695265 Book/CD Pack $15.99

Latin Bass
by George Lopez and David Keif • Private Lessons
00695543 Book/CD Pack $15.99

Music Reading for Bass
by Wendy Wrehovcsik • Essential Concepts
00695203............................. $10.95

GUITAR

Advanced Guitar Soloing
by Daniel Gilbert & Beth Marlis • Essential Concepts
00695636 Book/CD Pack $19.95

Advanced Scale Concepts & Licks for Guitar
by Jean Marc Belkadi • Private Lessons
00695298 Book/CD Pack $16.95

Basic Blues Guitar
by Steve Trovato • Private Lessons
00695180 Book/CD Pack $15.99

Blues/Rock Soloing for Guitar
by Robert Calva • Private Lessons
00695680 Book/CD Pack $18.95

Blues Rhythm Guitar
by Keith Wyatt • Master Class
00695131 Book/CD Pack $19.95

Dean Brown
00696002 DVD....................... $29.95

Chord Progressions for Guitar
by Tom Kolb • Private Lessons
00695664 Book/CD Pack $16.95

Chord Tone Soloing
by Barrett Tagliarino • Private Lessons
00695855 Book/CD Pack $22.95

Chord-Melody Guitar
by Bruce Buckingham • Private Lessons
00695646 Book/CD Pack $16.95

Prices, contents, and availability subject to change without notice.
For More Information, See Your Local Music Dealer, Or Write To:

HAL•LEONARD CORPORATION
7777 W. BLUEMOUND RD. P.O. BOX 13819 MILWAUKEE, WI 53213

www.halleonard.com

Classical & Fingerstyle Guitar Techniques
by David Oakes • Master Class
00695171 Book/CD Pack $16.95

Classical Themes for Electric Guitar
by Jean Marc Belkadi • Private Lessons
00695806 Book/CD Pack $15.99

Contemporary Acoustic Guitar
by Eric Paschal & Steve Trovato • Master Class
00695320 Book/CD Pack $16.95

Creative Chord Shapes
by Jamie Findlay • Private Lessons
00695172 Book/CD Pack $10.99

Diminished Scale for Guitar
by Jean Marc Belkadi • Private Lessons
00695227 Book/CD Pack $10.99

Essential Rhythm Guitar
by Steve Trovato • Private Lessons
00695181 Book/CD Pack $15.99

Ethnic Rhythms for Electric Guitar
by Jean Marc Belkadi • Private Lessons
00695873 Book/CD Pack $17.99

Exotic Scales & Licks for Electric Guitar
by Jean Marc Belkadi • Private Lessons
00695860 Book/CD Pack $16.95

Funk Guitar
by Ross Bolton • Private Lessons
00695419 Book/CD Pack $15.99

Guitar Basics
by Bruce Buckingham • Private Lessons
00695134 Book/CD Pack $17.95

Guitar Fretboard Workbook
by Barrett Tagliarino • Essential Concepts
00695712............................. $17.99

Guitar Hanon
by Peter Deneff • Private Lessons
00695321............................. $9.95

Guitar Lick•tionary
by Dave Hill • Private Lessons
00695482 Book/CD Pack $18.95

Guitar Soloing
by Dan Gilbert & Beth Marlis • Essential Concepts
00695190 Book/CD Pack $19.95
00695907 DVD....................... $19.95

Harmonics
by Jamie Findlay • Private Lessons
00695169 Book/CD Pack $13.99

Introduction to Jazz Guitar Soloing
by Joe Elliott • Master Class
00695406 Book/CD Pack $19.95

Jazz Guitar Chord System
by Scott Henderson • Private Lessons
00695291............................. $10.95

Jazz Guitar Improvisation
by Sid Jacobs • Master Class
00695128 Book/CD Pack $18.99
00695908 DVD....................... $19.95
00695639 VHS Video $19.95

Jazz-Rock Triad Improvising
by Jean Marc Belkadi • Private Lessons
00695361 Book/CD Pack $15.99

Latin Guitar
by Bruce Buckingham • Master Class
00695379 Book/CD Pack $16.95

Modern Approach to Jazz, Rock & Fusion Guitar
by Jean Marc Belkadi • Private Lessons
00695143 Book/CD Pack $15.99

Modern Jazz Concepts for Guitar
by Sid Jacobs • Master Class
00695711 Book/CD Pack $16.95

Modern Rock Rhythm Guitar
by Danny Gill • Private Lessons
00695682 Book/CD Pack $16.95

Modes for Guitar
by Tom Kolb • Private Lessons
00695555 Book/CD Pack $17.95

Music Reading for Guitar
by David Oakes • Essential Concepts
00695192............................. $19.99

The Musician's Guide to Recording Acoustic Guitar
by Dallan Beck • Private Lessons
00695505 Book/CD Pack $13.99

Outside Guitar Licks
by Jean Marc Belkadi • Private Lessons
00695697 Book/CD Pack $15.99

Power Plucking
by Dale Turner • Private Lesson
00695962............................. $19.95

Practice Trax for Guitar
by Danny Gill • Private Lessons
00695601 Book/CD Pack $17.99

Progressive Tapping Licks
by Jean Marc Belkadi • Private Lessons
00695748 Book/CD Pack $15.95

Rhythm Guitar
by Bruce Buckingham & Eric Paschal • Essential Concepts
00695188 Book $17.95
00695644 VHS Video $19.95

Rock Lead Basics
by Nick Nolan & Danny Gill • Master Class
00695144 Book/CD Pack $17.99
00695910 DVD....................... $19.95

Rock Lead Performance
by Nick Nolan & Danny Gill • Master Class
00695278 Book/CD Pack $17.95

Rock Lead Techniques
by Nick Nolan & Danny Gill • Master Class
00695146 Book/CD Pack $15.95

Slap & Pop Technique for Guitar
00695645 Book/CD Pack $14.99

Technique Exercises for Guitar
by Jean Marc Belkadi • Private Lessons
00695913............................. $14.95

Texas Blues Guitar
by Robert Calva • Private Lessons
00695340 Book/CD Pack $17.95

Ultimate Guitar Technique
by Bill LaFleur • Private Lessons
00695863............................. $19.95

1109

GUITAR signature licks

Signature Licks book/CD packs provide a step-by-step breakdown of "right from the record" riffs, licks, and solos so you can jam along with your favorite bands. They contain performance notes and an overview of each artist's or group's style, with note-for-note transcriptions in notes and tab. The CDs feature full-band demos at both normal and slow speeds.

ACOUSTIC CLASSICS
00695864 ....$19.95

BEST OF ACOUSTIC GUITAR
00695640 ....$19.95

AEROSMITH 1973-1979
00695106 ....$22.95

AEROSMITH 1979-1998
00695219 ....$22.95

BEST OF AGGRO-METAL
00695592 ....$19.95

BEST OF CHET ATKINS
00695752 ....$22.95

THE BEACH BOYS DEFINITIVE COLLECTION
00695683 ....$22.95

BEST OF THE BEATLES FOR ACOUSTIC GUITAR
00695453 ....$22.95

THE BEATLES BASS
00695283 ....$22.95

THE BEATLES FAVORITES
00695096 ....$24.95

THE BEATLES HITS
00695049 ....$24.95

BEST OF GEORGE BENSON
00695418 ....$22.95

BEST OF BLACK SABBATH
00695249 ....$22.95

BEST OF BLINK-182
00695704 ....$22.95

BEST OF BLUES GUITAR
00695846 ....$19.95

BLUES GUITAR CLASSICS
00695177 ....$19.95

BLUES/ROCK GUITAR MASTERS
00695348 ....$21.95

KENNY BURRELL
00695830 ....$24.95

BEST OF CHARLIE CHRISTIAN
00695584 ....$22.95

BEST OF ERIC CLAPTON
00695038 ....$24.95

ERIC CLAPTON – THE BLUESMAN
00695040 ....$22.95

ERIC CLAPTON – FROM THE ALBUM UNPLUGGED
00695250 ....$24.95

BEST OF CREAM
00695251 ....$22.95

CREEDANCE CLEARWATER REVIVAL
00695924 ....$22.95

DEEP PURPLE – GREATEST HITS
00695625 ....$22.95

THE BEST OF DEF LEPPARD
00696516 ....$22.95

THE DOORS
00695373 ....$22.95

ESSENTIAL JAZZ GUITAR
00695875 ....$19.99

FAMOUS ROCK GUITAR SOLOS
00695590 ....$19.95

BEST OF FOO FIGHTERS
00695481 ....$24.95

ROBBEN FORD
00695903 ....$22.95

GREATEST GUITAR SOLOS OF ALL TIME
00695301 ....$19.95

BEST OF GRANT GREEN
00695747 ....$22.95

BEST OF GUNS N' ROSES
00695183 ....$24.95

THE BEST OF BUDDY GUY
00695186 ....$22.95

JIM HALL
00695848 ....$22.99

HARD ROCK SOLOS
00695591 ....$19.95

JIMI HENDRIX
00696560 ....$24.95

JIMI HENDRIX – VOLUME 2
00695835 ....$24.95

HOT COUNTRY GUITAR
00695580 ....$19.95

BEST OF JAZZ GUITAR
00695586 ....$24.95

ERIC JOHNSON
00699317 ....$24.95

ROBERT JOHNSON
00695264 ....$22.95

THE ESSENTIAL ALBERT KING
00695713 ....$22.95

B.B. KING – THE DEFINITIVE COLLECTION
00695635 ....$22.95

B.B. KING – MASTER BLUESMAN
00699923 ....$24.95

THE KINKS
00695553 ....$22.95

BEST OF KISS
00699413 ....$22.95

MARK KNOPFLER
00695178 ....$22.95

LYNYRD SKYNYRD
00695872 ....$24.95

BEST OF YNGWIE MALMSTEEN
00695669 ....$22.95

BEST OF PAT MARTINO
00695632 ....$22.95

WES MONTGOMERY
00695387 ....$24.95

BEST OF NIRVANA
00695483 ....$24.95

THE OFFSPRING
00695852 ....$24.95

VERY BEST OF OZZY OSBOURNE
00695431 ....$22.95

BEST OF JOE PASS
00695730 ....$22.95

PINK FLOYD – EARLY CLASSICS
00695566 ....$22.95

THE POLICE
00695724 ....$22.95

THE GUITARS OF ELVIS
00696507 ....$22.95

BEST OF QUEEN
00695097 ....$24.95

BEST OF RAGE AGAINST THE MACHINE
00695480 ....$24.95

RED HOT CHILI PEPPERS
00695173 ....$22.95

RED HOT CHILI PEPPERS – GREATEST HITS
00695828 ....$24.95

BEST OF DJANGO REINHARDT
00695660 ....$24.95

BEST OF ROCK
00695884 ....$19.95

BEST OF ROCK 'N' ROLL GUITAR
00695559 ....$19.95

BEST OF ROCKABILLY GUITAR
00695785 ....$19.95

THE ROLLING STONES
00695079 ....$24.95

BEST OF DAVID LEE ROTH
00695843 ....$24.95

BEST OF JOE SATRIANI
00695216 ....$22.95

BEST OF SILVERCHAIR
00695488 ....$22.95

THE BEST OF SOUL GUITAR
00695703 ....$19.95

BEST OF SOUTHERN ROCK
00695560 ....$19.95

ROD STEWART
00695663 ....$22.95

BEST OF SURF GUITAR
00695822 ....$19.95

BEST OF SYSTEM OF A DOWN
00695788 ....$22.95

ROBIN TROWER
00695950 ....$22.95

STEVE VAI
00673247 ....$22.95

STEVE VAI – ALIEN LOVE SECRETS: THE NAKED VAMPS
00695223 ....$22.95

STEVE VAI – FIRE GARDEN: THE NAKED VAMPS
00695166 ....$22.95

STEVE VAI – THE ULTRA ZONE: NAKED VAMPS
00695684 ....$22.95

STEVIE RAY VAUGHAN – 2ND ED.
00699316 ....$24.95

THE GUITAR STYLE OF STEVIE RAY VAUGHAN
00695155 ....$24.95

BEST OF THE VENTURES
00695772 ....$19.95

THE WHO – 2ND ED.
00695561 ....$22.95

BEST OF ZZ TOP
00695738 ....$24.95

FOR MORE INFORMATION,
SEE YOUR LOCAL MUSIC DEALER,
OR WRITE TO:

HAL•LEONARD CORPORATION
7777 W. BLUEMOUND RD. P.O. BOX 13819
MILWAUKEE, WISCONSIN 53213
www.halleonard.com

COMPLETE DESCRIPTIONS AND SONGLISTS ONLINE!
Prices, contents and availability subject to change without notice.